THE C FACTOR

The Common Cure For Your Capital Campaign Conundrums

By Patrick G. McLaughlin
Author of *Major-Donor Game Plan*

Enjoy the Book

its an overview of

our campaigns Around the

world "Blessings"

Pat - 2008

Psalm 127:1

Thanks to Jane, my wife and life partner, business partner, and best buddy. After 40 years of hanging out, it's still awesome.

To Seth, Renee, Matt, and Kristen, thanks, I once again used a few of those real family stories to illustrate a point or two.

To Donyo, Ronyo, Johnyo, and Howie, thanks for your recommendations and input as this project took shape.

Special thanks to Jean Bloom from Zondervan and Sarah Nunham from The Timothy Group who have been troopers again on this book.

Very special thanks to the 1,000+ clients I have been privileged to serve in their annual, capital, and endowment funding programs throughout the past 28 years. You have provided me the opportunity to work in the laboratory of real life, conducting nearly 300 capital campaigns and giving me insight, so together we could identify and solve most of those campaign conundrums.

P.S. Kent Power — Thanks a zillion!

Table of Contents

Foreword

I never cease to be amazed at the breadth of the knowledge base required to lead a non-public school or non-profit agency these days. The complexities of HR issues, recruiting personnel, meeting the expectations of our constituents, achieving the goals of our strategic plan, and performing up to our own standard of excellence can be formidable. Then along comes the need for a major capital campaign! Even those of us with extensive graduate-level training and many years on the job feel inadequate when confronted with the need for our school or our ministry to raise big bucks! Nothing makes a leader wearier than enduring prolonged periods of time feeling inadequate for the task ahead. Here's an opportunity to begin to address this need by learning from one of the most experienced leaders in the business.

When an athlete is preparing for the big game, there is great comfort in realizing that the coach has been there before, has a track record of success, and knows how to prepare for the challenge ahead. We have benefited greatly from our association with Pat McLaughlin throughout our capital campaign. His counsel and expertise have been great assets in enabling us to direct an effective capital effort. Having "Coach Pat" directing our team has also helped this headmaster sleep a little better at night!

The C Factor provides not only a biblically based, theoretically sound framework for thinking through the capital campaign, but it also provides practical "how to" direction for the overall process. These are not hypothetical strategies ready for a field test, but tried-and-true methods that can help you avoid the big mistakes and seize the opportunities that lie before you.

We recognize that "unless the Lord builds the house, they labor in vain..." The results of the campaign are ultimately in the Lord's hands. Doing our homework, working smarter not just harder, and taking advantage of the experience of a successful professional like Pat McLaughlin, however, are essential on our side of the equation. May the Lord bless your efforts in whatever campaign you undertake to advance His kingdom!

> Michael M. Sligh, Ed. D.
> Headmaster
> Lakeland Christian School
> Lakeland, Florida

Introduction

Every organization must raise money for these specific needs so it can move forward, grow, and stay healthy:

- *annual/operational funds* (what it takes to operate your organization each year)
- *endowment funds* (to help your organization ensure its future and to offset annual/operational funds for scholarships, endowed chairs, physical plant maintenance, etc.)
- *capital funds* (for new or expanded programs, personnel, and property)

The question isn't *if* your organization needs to plan and implement a capital campaign but *when.* You must plan for expansion. But come on, let's be honest. Every capital campaign since the beginning of time has experienced at least one conundrum. By my definition, a conundrum is a hitch in the get-a-long, a curve ball you didn't see coming, an unexpected breakdown, or a challenge or issue that must be addressed. So the campaign you are considering, are planning, or are currently running will probably hit a snag or two…or twenty-two!

Did you know the Bible is full of capital campaign conundrums? Moses conducted a capital campaign as recounted in Exodus 25, and that forty-year travail in the wilderness presented one big challenge after another. Nehemiah was ridiculed by his own countrymen in his capital campaign to rebuild the wall of Jerusalem. That was an internal conundrum, which can be especially painful. Haggai had to challenge all three audiences in his region—political rulers, religious leaders, and the common people—to overcome the conundrums in getting his capital project underway.

In slightly more modern times, Harvard College conducted one of the first campaigns in the new colonies and experienced its share of issues. But here is the most interesting one: Miami University in Ohio conducted a campaign and did not receive a final report for 127 years! No closure for 127 years and their chief advancement/fundraising officer also died in the line of duty. Can I hear someone say the word *conundrum*? (You'll hear more about these stories in chapter one).

If the conundrums in those campaigns could be worked out, then you can work out yours too. You can even try to avoid them! But how and when do you address capital campaign conundrums?

Working a jigsaw puzzle—like the ones with a thousand pieces your family puts together over Christmas break—

usually begins with assembling border pieces and then placing interior pieces. But sometimes it all goes wrong. You did it right with the border pieces; they fit perfectly. But some of the interior pieces just don't seem to fit—a conundrum! So do you try to force the pieces to somehow fit, or do you study the picture on the box, refocus, and then go to work with a better idea of how to proceed? (And could you have avoided this conundrum if you had studied the picture on the puzzle box in the first place?)

The C Factor was written to help you who are considering, planning, or currently running a capital campaign to discover the common cure for capital campaign conundrums. We'll cover twelve basic campaign principles, the four phases of a capital campaign, the importance of board involvement, and campaigning with volunteers, all the while on the watch for conundrums that can be fixed or even avoided. And you'll see that I incorporate certain conundrum-freeing concepts more than once because they are just that important.

So are you ready to dive in and lead your organization through an exciting and successful capital campaign with as few conundrums as possible? Then please read on. Whether conundrums are already frustrating your efforts or you want to avoid as many of them as possible as you plan a campaign, this book is for you.

And why *not* shoot for a conundrum-*free* campaign?

Pat McLaughlin
Summer 2007

1

Capital Campaign Conundrums through the Ages

"We're on a mission from God."
— Elwood Blues

"I am doing a great work and I cannot
come down." — Nehemiah

I believe in our Timothy Group clients, and I have put my shoulder to the plow to help them fulfill their visions over the years. But I readily admit that I have experienced conundrums in that process.

Beginning with a campaign almost fifteen hundred years before the birth of Christ, you are about to take a brief, whirlwind tour of a few capital campaigns *way* before my time. And as you'll see from these historical examples, it's not likely that many campaigns throughout the history of mankind have been conundrum-free.

The Ultimate Vision Statement for a Mobile Worship Center (1491 B.C.)

In *The Blues Brothers* movie, Jake Blues gets a vision to save the orphanage where he and his brother, Elwood, grew up by putting their band back together. The vision comes to him in, of all places, a church. When our clients tell us they are on a mission from God, they almost sound like what happened to Jake in the movie happened to them: "God gave us the vision to launch this effort. We have created our vision statement and are convinced it is a directive from God."

Well, Moses did have an ultimate directive from God when God spoke to him in person. In Exodus 24, we learn that Moses spent forty days and nights with God in a cloud on a mountain. There was so much smoke and awe that Aaron and the men who took the journey with Moses did not make the climb. It was just God and Moses up there, having a chat about the need and details for a mobile worship center to be called the tabernacle.

Now, I am not sure if any other campaign in history got a vision as directly from God, though perhaps all of us planning campaigns should at least spend forty days and nights communicating with God to make sure our vision matches His. But with that divine vision clearly in mind, Moses and Aaron conducted one of the first capital campaigns recorded. Moses came down from the mount and told the wilderness sojourners about the tabernacle. The children of Israel bought into the plan and vision for a couple of reasons. Reason number one was that Moses' face glowed as the glory of God was still upon him. Reason number two was that a few times, when they didn't believe and follow orders, the earth opened up and ate some of them for lunch. Yes, they disappeared from the face of the earth. I think this is a great reason to get excited about a capital campaign.

A Vision from God

In my book *Major-Donor Game Plan*[1], I write about how Moses started at the top in sharing this vision. In Exodus 25:1, he told the people about the need to give so they could build this visionary mobile worship center. He asked leaders and high-capacity donors at the top of the economic scale upfront to give gifts of gold, silver, and bronze. Then

Moses and Aaron worked their way down through several million people (the other giving units) and gave everyone the opportunity to buy into this unique vision. We know the plan was successful because, by Exodus 36, Moses had brought the campaign to fulfillment and announced they had reached their goal.

> So Moses gave the command, and this message was sent throughout the camp: "Men and women, don't prepare any more gifts for the sanctuary. We have enough!" So the people stopped bringing their sacred offerings. Their contributions were more than enough to complete the whole project (Exodus 36: 6-7 NLT).

What an encouraging announcement for those who had thought there were too many conundrums to complete the capital project! No doubt Moses also made a final campaign report to the leaders, showing how the campaign had been a success. It's amazing that Moses could make a report without a desk-top publishing program or a cool PowerPoint presentation, but whatever campaign conundrums existed, I think he and Aaron clearly articulated the vision and then worked out any and all conundrums with the resources they had. And then they actually told the people to stop giving. Has that ever happened at your organization?

...[Moses] and Aaron clearly articulated the vision and then worked out any and all conundrums...

The Kitchen Steward Leads a
Major Campaign (445 B.C.)

Nehemiah, the kitchen steward for King Artaxerxes at the palace in Susa, was an unlikely capital campaign director. His life was full of conundrums as he was a slave, a captive Hebrew working for a gentile king. He befriended the king, and I truly believe Artaxerxes trusted and respected Nehemiah, who hired all the cafeteria staff for the palace. When the king got hungry in the middle of the night, it was Nehemiah he woke up to prepare a snack and taste it to make sure no one had poisoned the food.

Yes, a great way to make a permanent change in your local monarch was to poison his food. But to do so you would have to bribe or manipulate the kitchen/cafeteria steward. Nehemiah, a man of great integrity, was neither bribed nor manipulated. So the king literally trusted Nehemiah with his life. Those late-night snacks of cold lamb on pita bread with a little Dijon mustard were very special times for the king and the slave. I envision these two night owls munching away, discussing the news, weather, and sports of the day. Over a twenty-year period they built a relationship, and, do I dare say, a friendship. Why do I think that? Because only a friend would recognize the change in Nehemiah's countenance and address it.

Nehemiah got word from back home that the walls and gates of Jerusalem were still in ruin. Many years after it should have been rebuilt and restored the city was still in complete chaos. When Nehemiah got the news, he was sad. "When I heard this, I sat down and wept. In fact, for days I mourned, fasted, and prayed to the God of heaven" (Nehemiah1:4 NLT).

"Vision begins with a holy discontent with the way things are," says English Theologian John R. W. Stott. Nehemiah began to form a holy vision in his mind and heart. It gripped him, and I dare say it consumed him. For when he served the king his next meal, his friend Artaxerxes noticed his visible sadness, his holy discontent.

> I was serving the king his wine. I had never before appeared sad in his presence. So the king asked me, "Why are you looking so sad? You don't look sick to me. You must be deeply troubled" (Nehemiah 2:1b-2 NLT).

Remember this historical perspective: Nehemiah was so consumed by his vision that he even took it to the office. Nehemiah answered the king this way:

> "Long live the king! How can I not be sad? For the city where my ancestors are buried is in ruins, and the gates have been destroyed by fire." The king asked, "Well, how can I help you?" (Nehemiah 2:3-4a NLT)

Then with a prayer to the God of heaven, Nehemiah replied:

> "If it please the king, and if you are pleased with me, your servant, send me to Judah to rebuild the city where my ancestors are buried." Then the king, with the queen sitting beside him, asked, "How long will

you be gone? When will you return?" After I told him how long I would be gone, the king agreed to my request (Nehemiah 2:5-6 NLT).

Nehemiah's campaign began to unfold from the minute he learned about the need back home for a big bricks and mortar capital fundraising effort. But talk about conundrums. He was living in captivity miles away from home, and he had a full-time job with no

> *...because of his friendship with the one and only major donor he knew personally, he was able to address four major needs...*

vacation time, no money, and no influence except on his kitchen staff. He needed to overcome a number of conundrums from the get-go for this project to have any chance of success. But because of his friendship with the one and only major donor he knew personally, he was able to address four major needs (or conundrums):

1. Time off from work (he got an extended vacation package)
2. Safe passage between the kingdoms (the king wrote a personal letter)
3. Royal timber (he got wall rebuilding material to take along)
4. A crew of soldiers and laborers (for protection and to help in this effort)

Nehemiah and his traveling capital campaign troop showed up and began to rebuild the wall. Then it happened.

Sanballat was very angry when he learned that we were rebuilding the wall. He flew into a rage and mocked the Jews, saying in front of his friends and the Samarian army officers, "What does this bunch of poor, feeble Jews think they're doing? Do they think they can build the wall in a single day by just offering a few sacrifices? Do they actually think they can make something of stones from a rubbish heap—and charred ones at that?" Tobiah the Ammonite, who was standing beside him, remarked, "That stone wall would collapse if even a fox walked along the top of it!" (Nehemiah 4:1-3 NLT)

The wall was rebuilt with money, equipment, material, and laborers from a gentile king a couple of kingdoms away. But in spite of this obvious miracle, Nehemiah experienced rejection, jealousy, envy, and strife. Are you ready? This treatment came from his own people, the folks for whom he was rebuilding the wall to improve their life and safety. Nehemiah seemingly had been blessed with one of the greatest miracles of all time, yet his own countrymen were critical. King Artaxerxes had inherited the throne from his father and from his father's father. He totally bought into Nehemiah's case for support, to rebuild the walls of his father's city and to restore a bit of his heritage. The king was on board, and Nehemiah was in tune.

But how about these Judeans who knew the wall needed to be rebuilt? They were jealous, envious, mean-spirited, and just flat out uninformed. Perhaps just down right stupid is the best description. Even after the wall was finished, they still wanted to meet Nehemiah and kill him (6:2). I love his message back to them in 6:3: "I am engaged in a great work, so I can't come. Why should I stop working to come and meet with you?" (NLT)

Instead of working for Nehemiah and his crew, these people chose to work against them. We know from Psalm 127:1 that it is all God's work: "Unless the LORD builds a house, the work of the builders is wasted. Unless the LORD protects a city, guarding it with sentries will do no good" (NLT). The conundrum here is that sometimes those who should most appreciate your hard work on a campaign do not. Yes, we all understand it's God's work, but just a bit of appreciation and cooperation may have made Nehemiah's capital campaign task a bit lighter.

David and Solomon Conduct a Campaign— The Temple of the Lord (1015 B.C.)

Even though David was blessed by God throughout his life, he experienced a number of personal and professional conundrums over the years. Stuff like murder, deceit, adultery, escaping for his life a few times—you know, just a handful of small sins and troubles. But David also had many victories. His defeat of the 9'6" giant named Goliath at age twelve or thirteen impacted an entire nation and led the Israelites to victory over the Philistines. His replacing

Saul as the king and leader of Israel led the nation to many great victories as well. David was a man after God's own heart, as evidenced by Jehovah's call upon his life to build the temple. Late in life, David did regain the joy of his salvation, which he requested in Psalm 51.

Now here was a call from Jehovah to fulfill Scripture by building a worship center to encourage, unite, and inspire the entire nation of God. God used both David and his successor and son, Solomon. David was handing the baton to Solomon. In I Chronicles 28:19-20 it is clear that David understood the plan and challenged the leaders to help Solomon.

> "Every part of this plan," David told Solomon, "was given to me in writing from the hand of the LORD." Then David continued, "Be strong and courageous, and do the work. Don't be afraid or discouraged, for the LORD God, my God, is with you. He will not fail you or forsake you. He will see to it that all the work related to the Temple of the LORD is finished correctly" (NLT).

A massive capital campaign effort—in either 1015 B.C. or now—is a God-sized task. David understood how big the task was and also knew he would not be around to help it come to fruition. (Great point here: If your CEO is leaving, they need to make sure their successor both has the same authority and approval they had and understands the size of the task.)

These principles seem evident in the life and stewardship practices (the temple campaign) of David, and ultimately in the life of his son, Solomon.

1. David gave first (I Chronicles 29:1-5)
2. David gave sacrificially (I Chronicles 29:2-3)
3. David gave publicly (I Chronicles 29:1-5)
4. David motivated others to give generously (I Chronicles 29:3-5)
5. David challenged others with a direct "ask" (I Chronicles 29:5)
6. David gave freely (I Chronicles 29:9,17)
7. David found joy in giving, as did others (I Chronicles 29:9-20)

David was a great warrior and leader, and had formed an extraordinary degree of national unity and purpose. Solomon would prove to be quite different from his father. He was not a warrior but a king who displayed his leadership gifts in the areas of administration, business, and trade. At enormous expense, Solomon built the great temple in Jerusalem, which was to become a central symbol of Israel's faith.

> *A massive capital campaign effort...is a God-sized task.*

How about you? Did your last capital campaign unify a nation? Mine didn't either. Solomon, inspired by his father, built one of the great wonders of the then-known world, and ruled over the united kingdom of Israel for forty years. Of all his great leadership and wisdom, his greatest accomplishment was this massive capital project, the building of the temple.

A Shepherd Leads a National Capital Campaign (520 B.C.)

This is my chance to put in a good word for the book of Haggai, the book of the Bible my friend Howard Dayton of Crown Ministries turned me on to in the late 80's. It is the second shortest book in the Old Testament, and it gets very little "preach time." Many people don't even know where it is in the Bible. As I often say, Haggai is in the clean part of your Bible. These thirty eight, power-packed verses remain somewhat unknown. But let me assure you that Haggai, a shepherd who is also somewhat unknown, experienced his share of conundrums in getting his campaign underway. In fact, his society had conundrums before they even had a campaign with conundrums!

Haggai rose up with a powerful message from Jehovah and challenged the children of Israel to get their proverbial act together. Fifty thousand Jewish citizens had returned to their regular lives from captivity in Babylonia. You know, buying, selling, trading, growing crops, raising sheep and cattle, raising children—all the mundane stuff of life. (Note: this is true, except for the raising of children, which can hardly be called mundane in any generation.) Anyway, they were living their lives back home with one major conundrum: they had not taken the time to rebuild the temple. It was still in ruins from their past battles and subsequent defeat at the hands of the Babylonians. Good news is usually fun to share, bad news as a general rule is not. But Haggai cranks up this message for the people of the day.

Then the LORD sent this message through the prophet Haggai: "Why are you living in luxurious houses while my house lies in ruins? This is what the LORD of Heaven's Armies says: Look at what's happening to you! You have planted much but harvest little. You eat but are not satisfied. You drink but are still thirsty. You put on clothes but cannot keep warm. Your wages disappear as though you were putting them in pockets filled with holes! This is what the LORD of Heaven's Armies says: Look at what's happening to you!" (Haggai 1:3-7 NLT)

Haggai helped them overcome the many conundrums that impacted every aspect of life ....

How is that for setting the stage for a great campaign, with bad news going from Haggai's (the capital campaign director) lips into every segment of society? Things are not going very well; in fact, things are disastrous. Want to fix all those conundrums? Let's launch a national capital campaign and rebuild the temple.

Then Haggai (speaking, of course, for God) said, "Now go up into the hills, bring down timber, and rebuild my house. Then I will take pleasure in it and be honored, says the LORD" (Haggai 1:8 NLT).

Oh, by the way, did I mention that he addressed the entire culture—political, social, religious, economic, and everyone in between? He spoke to the king and princes just like he spoke to the Levites and to the common man. The message was the same to everyone in the country of Judea: "We have an elephant in the room and we need to address it because this conundrum is impacting every thread in the fabric of our society and culture." He was straight-up honest and shared an unpopular message no one wanted to hear. (If that is what it takes to get your capital campaign up and moving, are you willing to address your administration, faculty, staff, trustees, and major donors in a "tough love" style? It can be risky business, but the result of Haggai's message was nothing shy of miraculous.)

God got their attention with some assistance from Haggai, pointing out the conundrums that had befallen the society and economy as a result of their focus on their own personal agendas. And then He made some unbelievable promises. He promised to bless their crops, their land, and their borders. He promised to bless them in battle. He guaranteed their success in Haggai 2:22 (NLT): "I will overthrow royal thrones and destroy the power of foreign kingdoms. I will overturn their chariots and riders. The horses will fall, and their riders will kill each other." The people got the campaign underway to rebuild the temple, and they all came together to ensure the project got done, finishing the temple in six months.

Haggai closed the book with another great promise in 2:23b (NLT): "I will honor you, Zerubbabel son of Shealtiel, my servant. I will make you like a signet ring on my finger, says the LORD, for I have chosen you. I, the LORD of Heaven's Armies, have spoken!"

Haggai helped the Israelites overcome the many conundrums that impacted every aspect of life for the Israelites. He helped them see the error of their ways and rebuild the temple. Would you want to be so honored by God that He proudly displayed you like a signet ring to show His delight in your capital campaign?

America's First Capital Campaign— Harvard College Builds (1641)

The history of fundraising campaigns in America has its roots in Harvard College and, through it, back in England. In 1641 the Massachusetts Bay colony sent three clergymen on a mission to raise capital monies for Harvard College. Reverend William Hibbens took a trip by ship to England. He returned to the colonies within a year with £500 for the college and more followed.[2]

The Reverends Thomas Weld and Hugh Peter stayed in England longer and continued to attempt to raise money. They wrote back early in their trip, requesting literature that would place Harvard College and New England in a positive light. The result was the "New England First Fruits Campaign," and the first attempt at a case statement/capital campaign brochure. The twenty-six-page tract set forth the purpose of the first American college and the importance the Puritans placed on education. Here is a quote from the document:

The result was...the first attempt at a case statement/capital campaign brochure.

After God had carried us safe to New England, and we had built our houses, provided necessaries for our livelihood, reared convenient places for Godly worship and settled the civil government: one of the next things we longed for and looked after was to advance learning and perpetuate it to prosperity: dreading to leave an illiterate ministry to the churches, when our present ministers shall lie in the dust. And as we were thinking and consulting how to effect this great work; it pleased God to stir up the heart of one Mr. Harvard (a Godly gentleman and lover of learning, there living amongst us), to give one half of his estate (it all being £1,700) towards the erecting of a college and library (a place very pleasant and accommodating) and is called according to the name of the first founder Harvard College.[3]

In addition to the support for the college, Weld and Peter sought gifts for the poor and for evangelizing Indians. The Harvard College fundraisers provided a fairly typical, tactical approach to fundraising for higher education in colonial America. Often the college would hire an agent or send the president on a mission to beg on behalf of Harvard. Because wealth was not abundant in the colonies, England was frequently targeted as a source of philanthropy. Sears reported, "The colonial colleges had many friends in the mother country."[4]

Later, George Whitefield, the famed pastor and evangelist, was the fundraiser of the day in the colonies. In his revivals of the 1730's and 1740's he passed the plate at his evangelistic rallies and church services. He often collected funds for poor debtors, the church, and the early colleges.

Perhaps George passed the plate early and often as is still practiced by some churches today. If I were to make an educated guess, this proved at times to be a conundrum if the plate was most often passed just one time per service.

After Harvard's founding in 1636, two other colleges were established over the next seventy-five years—Princeton, by the Presbyterians William and Mary in Virginia, and Yale in Connecticut. All the early colleges received grants and annual subventions by the King of England or by their provincial governments. Both of these funding sources proved, however, to be woefully inadequate. Sound similar to your situation today? The colleges survived because of broad-based interest of educated citizens who had the capacity to make small and large gifts to the colleges.[5]

For the well-to-do in those early days, solicitation was personal, using a typical pledge methodology. They were often asked for a specific amount over a specific period of time. The lower classes were solicited through lotteries, whose profits accrued to the colleges. As mentioned previously, much of the money raised in those campaigns was raised in England. Other notable firsts in the area of campaigns came from Lady Mowlson of England, who established the first scholarship at Harvard in 1643, and Thomas Hollis of England, who provided the first professorship of Divinity for Harvard in 1721.[6]

To summarize, capital fundraising in the American colonies often took the form of a subscription (a signed promise). This was also the advent of the early "letter of intent," or signed commitment card. Through the request of the churches, town officials would set aside a day when every citizen would be asked to make a subscription (pledge) to the college in their area. Those lists were published, and it was considered desirable to have one's name appear on the list of college patrons.

It is not difficult to see historical perspectives in this story that are still part of capital campaigns today. I am confident there were conundrums; imagine living in a small village and deciding you did not want to participate on "pledge day." Ouch, was it the stocks, a flogging, or perhaps some other form of public punishment and shame? There's a conundrum for certain.

Miami University (Ohio)— The 127-Year Campaign (1810)

We think five-year campaigns are lengthy in our modern fundraising culture. How about a 127-year campaign that was full of conundrums from the beginning? Miami College at Oxford, Ohio, received its charter in 1810 and immediately got into the fundraising business. Reverend John H. Browne was hired by the college that same year to travel east and raise capital to build a library, the first building on campus. Rev. Browne's adventure turned out to be the longest campaign in the history of higher education campaigning, 127 years between the kick-off and presentation of his final report. Did I hear

[It] turned out to be the longest campaign in the history of higher education campaigning, 127 years....

someone begin to slip the word *conundrum* through their lips? In fact, perhaps "mega" conundrum would be the best definition.

Rev. Browne traveled east by horseback to raise capital monies for a college in name only. All that existed was a township of wild, undeveloped land, and the "Act to Establish Miami University and a state appointed Board of Trustees."[7] Two Ohio senators helped Rev. Browne by donating $20 each, so the campaign was officially kicked off in 1810 with $40 in cash and pledges. On horseback, Rev. Browne continued to raise funds, collect books for the new library, and raise awareness for this new Ohio institution of higher learning. On a trip back to the college in 1812, he and his horse drowned while fording the Little Miami River. In all, the only results of Browne's efforts were a little more than $1,000 and many books.

In 1937, Samuel L. Stokes, a grandson of Rev. Browne, presented the president of Miami University with an envelope containing Rev. Browne's long-delayed report on the capital campaign, a report he completed before attempting to ford the river. Mr. Stokes had found the papers in a trunk that belonged to his grandmother.[8]

As these historical campaigns reveal, conundrums of all shapes and sizes impact efforts. Imagine yourself in all these situations. Your campaign agent dies and you do not receive the final report for 127 years; you employ three campaign agents and only one of them ever returns to campus; you are in captivity and your boss helps you but the people who should most appreciate the campaign attempt to kill you.

We could go on and on, but we know that campaigns

conducted throughout the history of the world had a conundrum or two somewhere in the process. It's not always about planning or campaign execution; sometimes it's just about people or the art form (not the science form) of any campaign. People make commitments of their time, talent, and treasure, and then sometimes they need to retract that commitment for a very good reason. Or those you are helping the most in a campaign turn against the project.

Yes, history tells us there have been very few, if any, conundrum-free capital campaigns, even in those that were ultimately successful. But, gratefully, we can learn from the past. Let's look at some more recent campaigns and see what else we can learn.

2

A Collection of Campaign Conundrums

"We made too many wrong mistakes."
— Yogi Berra

"When mistakes occur, redirect the energy." — Ken Blanchard

After twenty eight years and more than one thousand clients, I knew The Timothy Group was an ideal source for researching campaign conundrums. We have conducted conundrum-free or nearly conundrum-free campaigns over the past eighteen years. But we still have stories to tell, many from our own experience and others from asking organizations if they have a campaign conundrum to share.

It's ideal to walk a client through all the phases of a

campaign. But sometimes organizations begin a campaign themselves and then decide to call for counsel when a plethora of conundrums have their campaigns stuck in neutral or in reverse. Trust me, I have been there and done that with clients. Obviously, we will not reveal their identities to protect the innocent and—in some cases—the guilty. But there are some unbelievable capital campaign stories out there in the non-public, 501 (C) 3 sector.

Three Ground Breakings Later, Still No Buildings

A potential client called and invited me to look over a capital project that was stuck in neutral. They were a twenty-five-year-old Christian school moving from a church campus to a new fifty-five-acre campus. The campus was debt-free, and most of the underground construction (water, sewer, fiber optics) was completed. No question that they were ready to go, but they had not raised the money to fulfill the second phase of the campus project, "the build out." They had not conducted a pre-campaign study, and they had not organized a campaign committee/team. They did have a very simple brochure but it certainly did not look like a brochure that would support a $15,000,000 campaign. They were discouraged, disoriented, and not sure of anything, except that they did not want to break ground again until they were ready—and I mean really ready—to build.

Oh, by the way, if you missed it in the subhead, allow me to remind you. *They had already scheduled and executed three groundbreaking events but had no buildings.* Yes, on three different occasions they had invited parents, the community, and the media to attend a groundbreaking. Apparently, a part of their campaign strategy was to break ground so people would believe they were really going to do this and start giving money to help them turn their goal into a reality. Three groundbreakings and not one building coming up out of the ground. In fact, I saw on my first visit to their pristine campus with no buildings that the sign had blown down in a wind storm a week or so earlier and no one had been out to get it back up. You know, the "Future Home of (name of school)" sign.

3 Ground Breakings and No Building

My concern for the school was multifaceted. I was concerned about the handful of donors who had already contributed but had not seen the project move forward. I was frankly concerned about the integrity of the school's brand. What do you say to new and existing donors who have helped you purchase the property and attended all three groundbreakings? What is your message to prospective new students and their parents? My future research would confirm that there was some major disbelief in the community surrounding this project. Three groundbreakings without a building on the campus begs the question, are the school leaders lunatics or liars? Well, they were neither, and we will get to the solution later in the book.

Our immediate goal was to identify the conundrum that was preventing the school from moving forward. Three visible, planned, community-wide groundbreaking events to inform all of your audiences should say you are serious about building a new campus (this time), but it never happened. You can only cry wolf so many times and then everyone stops listening. Your message is muted by your inability to deliver on your promises.

What do you say to new and existing donors who have helped you purchase the property and attended all three groundbreakings?

CONUNDRUM: A conundrum developed when no one raised a hand in a board or campaign meeting to ask how the campaign was supposed to be conducted and if breaking ground a second and third time would really cause people to give money to the project. The answer would have been no! It was bad strategy to assume that breaking ground would cause people to begin to give money. Obviously, they had no solid campaign plan to raise one half to two thirds of the campaign goal ($7.5-$10 million) before going public with a groundbreaking. There was also no time line to help manage the events and flow of a twelve- to thirty-six-month campaign.

Great Full-Color Brochure, but . . .

A new client brought The Timothy Group in for a sit down planning meeting with their entire capital campaign committee. I invested a few hours in listening to their suc- cesses and conundrums to date, and reviewed their col- lateral materials. They had a beautiful 14 page, full-color campaign brochure, and two really nice newsletters. The campaign goal was $3 million and they were announcing that they had one third of their goal in cash and 3-year commitments. Here was the breakdown: $250,000 in new cash and commitments and $750,000 from the sale of a piece of property that had been donated to the organiza- tion.

That is a grand total of $1 million. It appeared to be a good project, they had the need for expanded facilities and their board and campaign team seemed passionate about the project. Their administrator was well respected and had been in place for 17 years.

Our goal for my first visit was to determine why this campaign was stuck in neutral and had only raised $250,000 (in new monies) in 16 months. After a couple of hours with the board and committee/team it became evident that they truly believed their beautiful full-color campaign brochure and newsletters were the keys to campaign success. Based upon our experience, the 14 page brochure was too long and there was no scale of gifts showing the breakdown of their $3 million need. It was very nice material but there was also no "ask"; it was "heavenly hinting" at its best.

Every fund raising document needs a trigger mechanism. It needs to share the number and size of gifts that are needed and invite the potential donor to give one of those gifts. As a result of not showing a scale of gifts, their largest gift to date in the campaign had been $30,000. In a normal campaign you would love a lead gift to be 10% of your campaign goal, not 1%. Obviously the $30,000 was a part of the $250,000 in new monies that had been raised. But keep in perspective that they only raised $250,000 of a $3 million campaign goal in the previous 16 months. The other $750,000 was from the sale of the property. We all asked, why?

When I brought it up at a meeting of the campaign committee/team the brochure designer—who was a member of the committee/team—became very defensive. (After the meeting I discovered he had been negative with most everyone on the committee/team.) In defending his beautiful brochure and newsletters he missed the most critical issue: Brochures, no matter how well conceived, do not raise money, especially if there is not a compelling financial request, a clear, straightforward ask to give financially over and above the current level of giving. For over a year this committee/team was not able to even articulate their frustration about the small amount of money raised with the existing campaign material.

CONUNDRUM: Full-color brochures do not raise money. People raise money. The conundrum was extended for eighteen months by inviting the designer of the campaign material to serve on the campaign committee/team. The defensive posture of this individual impacted many of the monthly campaign meetings. The conundrum was exacerbated by the committee's/team's feeling they could not have an objective conversation regarding the material without an argument. There was an elephant in the room no one would address because of the potential of a blow up. The largest conundrum of all was the lack of an ask, a financial request, and no scale of gift based upon the campaign need. We cannot expect our donors to do the math and figure out the giving chart. Brochures are about education; a personal visit is all about solicitation.

New Campaign Development Officer without Training or a Mentor

A Christian school employed a parent to take on the director of development position. "Sam" was a former business person who knew the business community, knew the school families well, had good verbal and writing skills, and was eager to make a positive impact on the school's need for new financial resources. But unsure about how to conduct a comprehensive campaign, Sam took a board member up on an offer to teach Sam everything the latter knew. The board member researched, wrote, and submitted requests for a variety of governmental agencies and agreed to help begin to research and present foundation proposals.

Over the course of the first eight months, Sam researched and submitted 182 foundation proposal requests, while the board member helped with research and continued to encourage Sam to keep at it and remain faithful. Dollars would surely begin to flow. Well, at long last the dollars did begin to flow (though *trickle* might be a better word), and the school finally received its one and only foundation grant. I hope you are sitting down. They received only one positive response with a one-time gift for $100. Just to be sure I had understood, I confirmed this in writing and in person. The school received 181 rejection letters and calls and one yes letter for $100. Sam told me they did not even recover their postage costs for the other 181 mailed requests.

Obviously, they needed to look at other forms of fundraising, and the foundation market was not a good fit with their short- and long-term fundraising goals. The campaign got off to a very slow start but has now recovered with a more comprehensive approach to a broader fundraising market.

CONUNDRUM: Sam needed comprehensive training and mentoring from a development/stewardship professional with a sound, twelve-month plan based upon good fundraising strategy to achieve the goals of the capital campaign. Foundation giving last year in America was between four and five cents of the non-profit dollar. The well-meaning board member did not mentor the development person well by helping with a flawed fundraising strategy. A comprehensive fundraising plan usually involves five fundraising methods applied to five target markets.

A Strategic Planning Weekend
Reveals Major Issues

Some years ago, I agreed to assist a client with a strategic planning weekend for a church board and a school board. The school functioned under the authority and 501 (C) 3 status of the church. The board retreat was scheduled for 6:00 p.m. to 10:00 p.m. on Friday evening and 8:00 a.m. to 2:00 p.m. on Saturday. You know, review the existing mission statement, tweak the vision statement, and define the core values and key results. Conduct a SWOT analysis (strengths, weaknesses, opportunities, threats) and begin to establish some development goals as they readied themselves for a capital campaign. It is difficult to get too far down the road in a capital campaign without a good strategic plan for the overall ministry. They were up to it and it went pretty well on Friday evening. But Saturday morning was a whole different animal.

An hour or so into the Saturday morning session we had a brief break and were preparing to do the SWOT analysis. That's when a school board member asked me a funny question: "Pat, didn't you say we could be completely honest during this campaign planning weekend?" When I confirmed that, the board member turned to the pastor and said, "Pastor, I think you have a major lack of integrity, you are a liar, and if I did not know better I would think you were demon-possessed."

Wow, tell us how you really feel about all of this! As you can imagine, the members chose sides very quickly. It was the school board versus the church board, and the pastor was stuck somewhere in the middle. It was hot and heavy with a bit of shouting and the like. An assistant pastor from another church had bowed his head and was praying. I got everyone's attention, thanked the board member for helping us identify a two-thousand-pound gorilla in the room, and I did something I had never done before and have never done since. I read I Corinthians 13. You know, the passage on love. I encouraged them to pray and dismiss for the day, and I appointed the assistant pastor who had been praying to wrap up the meeting. I informed them I was leaving and that a strategic plan would not be written as a result of the meeting as originally planned. They were not ready for a plan, and I encouraged them to put the capital campaign on hold. I asked them to take a few weeks off to think and pray about the direction of the school, and I told them I would be back when they were ready.

CONUNDRUM: This group lacked a unified vision and agreement on how to implement a strategic ministry advancement plan. They had two very different perspectives (church and school) on the way forward with their polity, policy, and with the campaign. And prior to our planning session, they apparently had been unable to express real and felt personal and institutional needs. They weren't ready for a capital campaign.

A Six-Million-Dollar Request to the Wrong Person

Every capital campaign has a personality of its own. In the pre-campaign study and quiet/leadership phases, we attempt to identify and begin to research and romance do-nors we think have major and mega capacity. (See chapter 3 for the five R's— Research, Romance, Request, Recognition, and Recruitment.) Our goal for phases I and II for one organization was $16,000,000 and the goal for phase III was for $11,000,000 to build science, technology, and classroom facilities. State-of-the-art planning and architectural drawings were prepared for all of the buildings before each phase. A local foundation had given a $500,000 gift in a campaign five years earlier, and we encouraged its participation once again.

A meeting was scheduled with the foundation director, who oversaw this multi-million dollar foundation for a family living outside of the US. She was a hometown person, and she got very excited about the project. In fact, she said these very words: "You are at $10,000,000 in cash and pledges. It seems you need to raise an additional $6,000,000 and complete phases I-II and get ready for the science and technology building in phase III."

She recommended the amount, not us. I want to make that crystal clear. Our thought going in was to make a $2,000,000 request or a way-out-there request for $3,000,000 (one million a year for three years as it was a thirty-six-month campaign). She walked us through how she wanted the proposal to look and did everything but hand us the check. She indicated the benefactor would be in the States to review a handful of proposals in the next month. The foundation director brought the daughter of the benefactor to the location to look at what their previous investment had helped to build. The daughter also reviewed the plans for the new capital campaign and placed her seal of approval on the project and the funding request. Between the daughter and the foundation director, they virtually assured us of the gift.

Perhaps you know what this conundrum is going to be. The benefactor returned to the States for a semi-annual meeting. Not only was the request amount denied, the benefactor indicated there would be no gift at all. Remember, they had given $500,000 in the last campaign, but even a request for that amount was refused. Embarrassed and frankly perplexed, the foundation director could only

> *...the gatekeeper doesn't usually own the castle.*

deliver the bad news and apologize for leading all of us down a path that did not produce gift income. She explained that she totally overestimated her ability to sway the donor/benefactor. We were reminded once again that the gatekeeper doesn't usually own the castle.

CONUNDRUM: Whenever possible, you need to make a presentation to the final decision maker. Maintain and enhance the ongoing relationship with the local foundation director, yes, but strategize on how to make a personal presentation to the actual benefactor.

An Eight-Month Gap in the Campaign Process

The difference between a long foul ball and a home run is one simple factor: *timing*. An early commitment to a sensible time line is a critical factor for the success of every capital campaign. This timing factor was reintroduced to us when we were once again employed to clean up the results of a poorly implemented plan. (I, along with you, am beginning to identify a trend. Are we the "campaign fixers?" Why didn't they call us in the first place? I only wish I knew.)

In this case, campaign counsel who had been successful with a couple of local secular college campaigns had been on board for one year. But the campaign had not gone very far. A national political research firm had done the pre-campaign study. It was well done, but we would have asked a number of different questions to a very different demographic profile. So in all fairness to them, a couple of strikes were already working against this effort.

The organization sent out a number of major-donor packages and indicated they would be calling to set appointments in the next two to four weeks. In the downtime of shopping and employing counsel and ramping up the new—and may I say more effective—strategy, the campaign calendar was significantly jeopardized. Over eight months went by between mailing the original major-donor packages and beginning telephone and personal contacts. Needless to say to your development professional, member of the board, or campaign volunteer, timing is critical. They had lost some major donors in this lapse.

CONUNDRUM: This organization did not understand the importance of an effective capital campaign calendar. Waiting eight months instead of only two to four weeks to schedule appointments following the mailed packages created an integrity and credibility gap, and the opportunity to meet with some major donors selected for personal solicitation visits was lost.

Board Participation at Less Than 1 Percent

An organization wanted to conduct a capital campaign to address three critical areas of growth. They had a plan and had even put dollar figures to their plan. They needed to raise $8.1 million. They raised $1.5 million in annual/operational funds, and they had conducted small capital campaigns in the past. The organization knew they needed a comprehensive capital effort to involve their existing donor base and broaden their fundraising capacity to the local community. They also knew the first step in the capital campaign was to make their own commitments. After the board made their cash and pledge commitments, the total was just $13,000 (thirteen thousand dollars). Yes, I spelled it out so you wouldn't think this was a mistake in the book.

...timing is critical.

Board members are volunteers and perhaps are busy in a number of places, but come on! First, if one of the goals of the board is to be pacesetters, then the bar was set fairly low in this project. They were in serious violation of two of the five G's of board leadership: Godly leadership, Governance, Give of their own personal resources, Get others to give of their personal resources, or Get off the board. Their own giving appeared to be very low based upon the size of the stated campaign goal. Second, how would the staff and campaign team convince their friends and business and church contacts to step up and give generously when it appeared the board did not do so? In one campaign with a goal of $16,000,000, a $1.5 million donor made a great statement: "Let's find out who else has some skin in the game." I believe this donor did, in fact, have a lot of skin in the game. I do not believe the board members with only $13,000 in cash and three-year commitments had nearly enough skin in the game in that campaign.

CONUNDRUM: At a recent Christian Stewardship Association Summer Institute, I lectured for twenty hours on building an effective major-donor program. So I obviously believe major-donor participation is a huge need in a capital campaign. The board of your organization needs to step up and practice the previously mentioned five G's of board leadership. Yes, friends and neighbors, it should come as no surprise that your board of directors needs to lead in investing their time, their talent, and their treasure in your organization.

My stewardship partner at The Timothy Group, Dr. Howard Nourse, has made this statement for the past fifteen years: "You cannot expect others to do what you are not prepared to do yourself." How can you ask friends, donors, foundations, corporations, businesses, and churches to give generously to your campaign if you have not given sacrificially? It is not about equal giving but about equal sacrifice. Not all the board members of the many organizations we have served were people of wealth. But every board member does need to be a person of sacrifice with their time, talent, and personal financial resources. If your board can only contribute 1 percent of your campaign goal, perhaps the goal is way too large. The obvious conundrum is not setting appropriate goals that everyone feels are fair and doable based on donor and board capacity. You'll read more about the role of the board in chapter 8.

Conundrum-Free Campaigning

It's always easy to be an armchair quarterback and help others make the right call. But perhaps you can relate to some of these conundrums. We included this chapter so you can begin right away to do some "conundrum checks" in your organizational strategy. Does a real live US Grade A, conundrum-free campaign really exist?

The short answer is probably not. But the long answer is that, with hard work and a good, solid, time-tested plan, you may get very close to being conundrum-free in your campaign. All of us who have a multitude of campaigns under our belts realize that a campaign conundrum can sometimes sneak up and whack you over the head without warning. Who could have known that a $6 million leveraged ask would end up a zero? Who could even imagine a foundation funding strategy that would lead to 181 no's and one yes! Three groundbreakings and still no buildings—you have got to be kidding. A board expecting a community to rally around their favorite ministry's capital campaign, when they have very little skin in the game.

...one of the goals of the board is to be pacesetters...

These were real conundrums. I am not kidding. So read on, and let's see if we can help you conundrum-proof your current or future campaign.

3

Twelve Capital Campaign Principles

"It is surprising how much you can accomplish if you don't care who gets the credit." — Abraham Lincoln

A few years ago, Detroit's General Motors ran an advertising campaign telling us their new Oldsmobile was "not your father's Oldsmobile." Remember those commercials? The ads, attempting to reestablish GM as a progressive manufacturer, were merely another way of saying, "Hey, give us a try. We have changed. Your parents drove our cars, and we want you to drive an Olds as well." Are you ready? General Motors is not even *making* the Oldsmobile anymore. How is that for change?

Organizational change is a constant. Managing change

is even a part of the ongoing Non Governmental Organization (NGO), the new descriptor of the 501 (C) 3 not-for-profit organization. And as we rapidly approach the ol' double digits in the new millennium (2010), things are not only a-changin' at warp speed, but are impacting the way we plan and implement capital campaigns for church, parachurch, and metachurch organizations.

As a general rule we like to see a campaign address three areas of an organization's needs (with multiple appeals to major donors in particular): (1) program advancement, (2) personnel (new staff), and (3) property (new or upgraded ministry facilities). So as you can see, campaigns are conducted for annual, capital, and endowment funding needs, not just for bricks and mortar.

Let's look at twelve principles that can have an impact on all capital campaigns, conundrum-free or not.

Principle 1
The Real Benefit of a Capital Campaign Case for Support Is That It Tests the State of Your Case

From my perspective the real benefit of a capital campaign case for support is that you can use it to test the state of your case. If the case for support for your capital campaign is clear, compelling, and visionary, your donors will buy into your case and support it financially. And when donors buy into your organizational mission and campaign case for support, they will invest their time, talent, and treasure to help you succeed. You will gain their trust, understanding, and belief in your campaign as well as two distinct commodities: human resources (time and talent) and dollar resources (over and above capital dollars).

"Case statement" is a legal term. If you were required to appear in a court of law and prove your case for your organization's existence, what would you be able to substantiate? Think about how you might build your case for support for your capital campaign. Here is a brief case statement outline.

- ➤ History — What are the significant milestones in the life of your organization? (Founding date, expansion dates, when new ministries were added, etc.)
- ➤ Purpose — Whom do you serve? What need called you into existence? How do you meet that need? What is your impact or your effectiveness?
- ➤ Need — What pressing needs does your organization have? What should your future include? What will this accomplish? What needs will be met? How do these needs relate to your ministry goals? What period of time will be required to meet the needs?
- ➤ Programs — What specific programs carry out your mission statement? What is the focus of each program? What are the long-range objectives of each program?
- ➤ Personnel — What experience does your staff have in providing these types of programs? What will expanding your ministry mean to your staff?
- ➤ Equipment/Materials — What equipment, technology, and material challenges do you face for future programs?

➤ Facilities — Where will each program be carried out?
➤ Costs — What is the cost of the overall program? If you have more than one cost, specify each segment.
➤ Funding Plan — On what project or projects are you focusing? Where do you plan to get the funding?

Build the case, the human need that drives your organi-

...the real benefit of a capital campaign case for support is that you can use it to test the state of your case.

zation, and share with your donors what it will take to fulfill the goals of your capital campaign. By communicating your need you will test your overall "state of the case" for your entire organization. By aligning your case with the passion of your donors, you will lay the groundwork for a conundrum-free campaign.

Principle 2
The Real Benefit of a Pre-Campaign Study Is That It Measures the Weaknesses in Your Organizational Capacity More Than the Strengths

We have seen a number of failed campaigns over the years that were launched without pre-campaign studies. And after twenty eight years of stewardship experience, I am convinced that a study is a must for a comprehensive capital campaign (combination of annual, capital, and endowment funding needs). A study will help you decrease your potential for campaign conundrums by revealing your organization's weaknesses as well as its strengths. You want to understand these weaknesses so you can prayerfully and carefully address them.

Without a study, will you know if you have the appropriate number of staff to manage a campaign? If your donor software has the capacity to manage a multi-faceted, multi-year campaign? If your existing donor base is large enough to fulfill your campaign without impacting your annual/operational campaign? If there are any public relations/branding issues that could negatively impact your organization?

What you do not know can and will hurt you in your campaign planning. If you ask the right questions in your study you should be able to identify a number of weaknesses. Be afraid, be very afraid, of what you do not address on the front end of a campaign. These unaddressed weaknesses are conundrums in the making, so we strongly believe in the pre-campaign study.

A bonus is that you may identify more organizational strengths than weaknesses in your study. Here is the principle re-defined: to be successful in a campaign, build on your strengths but carefully address the identified weaknesses to decrease the potential for campaign failure. (In the next chapter we will give some very specific examples to further emphasize this principle.)

Let me share a real-life example of what a study can reveal. We have just completed a pre-campaign study for a national organization with local and regional ministry centers. A recurring issue was inexperienced leadership: a board with lack of influence and affluence and volunteers who

What you do not know can and will hurt you in your campaign planning.

are not willing to invest time, talent, and treasure. Another weakness that surfaced is a lack of major-donor partici- pation. The organization is well known and loved but the relationship with major do- nors is a surface relationship at best. Few in the community could identify the mission, vision, and core values of this seventy-five-year-old organization.

We did not feel a campaign was the best way to proceed at this time, and recommended instead that they enhance the board and embark on a one-year communication and education program to win over the community. And as we helped this organization address its weaknesses, their strengths became more evident.

Principle 3
The Best Time to Raise Capital Monies Is When You Need Them

Come on, Pat, you say. This surely cannot be an over- arching principle for conundrum-free campaigns. But if your organization does not have a real and felt *need* to raise capital dollars then your efforts are going to be a bit like pushing spaghetti uphill. I mean warm, wiggly soft spa- ghetti. It is going to be a tough sell to your donor audi- ences.

There is an incredible opportunity for raising funds, no question. With America rapidly approaching an annu- al, across-the-board giving plateau at three hundred billion dollars, plenty of resources are out there in the stewardship/ philanthropic marketplace. But there are also plenty of options for donors to invest their dollars. Many donors give to many organizations, so their loyalties are often broad.

Perhaps this is the most critical question you can ask internally: What do we really need to fund in our organization right now? If there is a split second of hesitation in your answer, perhaps your capital campaign—be it a church, parachurch, or metachurch effort—needs some additional planning. Have you created internal wants and needs lists? Have you asked the right questions of your leadership team, staff, volunteers, and customers or service recipients? If you had all the financial resources you needed, what would you do at your organization? Many capital campaign conundrums are self-induced. We just flat out fail to plan.

Yogi Berra, famed New York Yankee catcher, major league manager, and Aflac Insurance spokesperson, is often quoted when it comes to strategic planning. He said, "If you don't know where you are going you are liable to end up someplace else," and "When you come to a fork in the road, take it." Clearly conundrums in the making. Many an organization has launched down the wrong path because they did not

> *...conundrums are self-induced. We just flat out fail to plan.*

do their homework, their planning. If you ask the tough questions upfront you increase your chances for success by really determining if your plan is right and the time is right to raise capital dollars.

One more perspective on planning and identifying the best time to raise capital dollars comes from Sir John Harvey Jones. He made this profound statement on planning: "Planning is an unnatural process; it is much more fun to do something. And the nicest thing about not planning is that failure comes as a complete surprise rather than being preceded by a period of worry and depression."

And then, there's planning and there's strategic planning.

Principle 4
Your Campaign's Success Depends Upon the Quality of Your Strategic Planning Process

Organizations do not plan to fail; they just sometimes fail to plan. To state the obvious, strategic planning is a process every organization must do and do well to compete in the new millennium ministry marketplace. A campaign needs to focus on your organizational mission, vision, and core values. John Stott says that "vision begins with a holy discontent with the way things are." As you conduct strategic planning in your organization, clearly identify those areas of discontent.

Strategic planning is a military term. It has to do with battle plans. With 1,400,000 not-for-profit agencies seeking their position in the marketplace, I hope you believe in strategic planning. It's a very competitive climate out there, and strategic planning will help you position your organization to clearly share your story and plan a great capital campaign. It will allow you to identify your uniqueness and your "sweet spot," if you will. It will help you keep your message clear, concise, and visionary. Begin planning with mission, vision, core values, and desired key results. The chart on page 60 is a strategic planning outline that has been used to tweak or create the desired vision and future for your organization.

An honest SWOT (strengths, weaknesses, opportunities, and threats) analysis should be a major part of your strategic and campaign planning process. What are your organizational strengths? What do you do really well? What are those core competencies that define your organization?

Next identify your organizational weaknesses. What could you and should you be doing better? For every organizational strength you identify, there is often an or-

Conundrums begin to develop if we don't ask these questions upfront.

ganizational weakness on the other side of the coin. Your greatest strength may also be your greatest weakness.

Continue the SWOT analysis by clearly identifying your organizational opportunities. What is out there on your ministry horizon that you should be doing? Here are excellent questions for you to ponder as you begin to think and plan strategically to get ready for a capital campaign:

• If we went out of business tomorrow, would we really be missed?
• What segment of society would not be served or impacted or would be underserved if we ceased to exist?

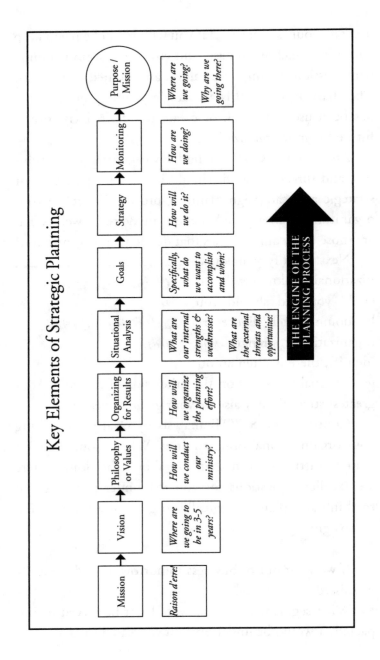

Key Elements of Strategic Planning

Mission	Vision	Philosophy or Values	Organizing for Results	Situational Analysis	Goals	Strategy	Monitoring	Purpose / Mission
Raison d'etre?	*Where are we going to be in 3-5 years?*	*How will we conduct our ministry?*	*How will we organize the planning effort?*	*What are our internal strengths & weaknesses?* *What are the external threats and opportunities?*	*Specifically, what do we want to accomplish and when?*	*How will we do it?*	*How are we doing?*	*Where are we going?* *Why are we going there?*

THE ENGINE OF THE PLANNING PROCESS

• Do we really need to act upon the opportunity now and is it a part of our strategic ministry plan?

Conundrums begin to develop if we don't ask these questions upfront.

And last, ask yourself what could become a threat to these very great "organizational opportunities." A financial threat? A staffing threat? A leadership threat? A donor threat? Ask yourself what could potentially derail, delay, or prevent your moving forward with funding your strategic plan with a successful capital campaign. You can minimize your threats and begin early to address campaign conundrums if you will carefully and prayerfully plan your work, then work your plan.

Here are some additional questions that could emerge in the strategic planning process.

1. What is needed and feasible in our service area?
2. What are we capable of doing well (core competencies)?
3. How will we do what we intend to do better?
4. Are our mission and vision clear to all of our audiences?
5. What will we be doing five years from now?
6. What might we not be doing five years from now?
7. Do we want to grow? If so, how large and why?
8. How will we accommodate our plans for growth?
9. If God answered one prayer about our organization's future, what would that one prayer and its answer be?

These questions are by no means exhaustive, but they will help you establish benchmarks for planning your conundrum-free capital campaign. The quality of strategic

planning has to do with the success of your campaign, so
get busy planning!

Principle 5
All Stewardship Dollars Flow on Trust but Big Capital
Dollars Rise to the Height of Organizational Vision

This principle is closely aligned with the previous two,
and clearly articulates the biblical principle that without vision the people perish. (Proverbs. 29:18 KJV) Wow, pretty
tough revelation. Do you think Solomon, who was one of
the wisest men who ever lived, is saying that without vision
we are going to die? Well, yes, as a matter of fact that is
exactly what he is saying.

Major donors in the US, Canada, the United Kingdom, and New Zealand—all places where we have worked
and conducted capital campaigns—indicate an interest in
funding *vision*. Most major donors who have the capacity to give big dollars have no interest in funding the past
(debt service), and frankly, most do not have much interest in helping you fund the present (annual/operational)
budget. Our experience and research indicate that major
donors want to help you make a difference in the future
(your organizational vision). I shared this concept in my
book *Major-Donor Game Plan*: The quality of your organizational and campaign vision will impact the quantity of
your major-donor participation.

If the 90/10 rule is a reality (90 percent of your capital campaign dollars may be given by 10 percent of your
donor constituency), it is imperative to clearly define and

re-define your vision statement. Write it in stone, shout it from the housetops, and make it known throughout your organization to all your target audiences. Haddon Robinson, former president of Denver Seminary, made this awesome statement regarding vision and how it grasps your constituents.

> *90 percent of your capital campaign dollars may be given by 10 percent of your donor constituency.*

"Leaders lift people's eyes to what matters. By bringing the eternal into time they summon Christians to a different perspective. Leaders must not only see the city; they must also talk about it in plain words their followers can grasp and that grasp their followers."

How high is your organizational vision? Is it high enough to grasp major and mega donors who have the capacity to help you achieve that vision? Lay out your strategy early and share these two elements with all of your target audiences: the uniqueness of your ministry (what sets you apart from others) and your organizational vision (where you are going and how you intend to get there).

Principle 6
A Successful Capital Campaign Is a Series of Small, Individual Campaigns Customized for No More Than Ten to One Hundred of Your Most Capable Donors

If you have not caught this yet, catch it now. Major donors can and will carry the day in your capital campaign. Bigger dollars add up faster. Five-figure gifts are very important to any campaign, and six-figure gifts are even more important. But seven-figure gifts really get you rolling toward campaign fulfillment.

Fifty-five-year-old Lakeland Christian School in Florida had never received a seven-figure gift. They created a strategic ministry plan, starting with defining their preferred future—what they wanted to build to ensure and enhance their future. There was some rolling of the eyes, and then they jotted down some huge numbers, almost ten times the dollar need from their previous campaign. The next step was to conduct a pre-campaign study to identify who might be able to give at the six- to-seven-figure level. They identified, asked for, and secured five seven-figure gifts and a number of six-figure contributions. Steve Wilson, the advancement director, and the campaign team secured two gifts of $2,000,000; three gifts of $1,000,000; two gifts of $500,000; and three gifts of $250,000. That is a very strong top-ten donor list!

Steve, headmaster Dr. Mike Sligh, and the campaign team did an excellent job of creating a series of small mini-campaigns designed specifically for select high-capacity donor prospects and suspects. Steve personalized material to the point of even including the names of children and grandchildren in some individual proposals. He even got inspired one evening and, by burning the midnight oil, created a personalized naming opportunity for a brand new million-dollar-capacity donor overnight. The proposal called for a naming opportunity for the donor and a very close friend who had helped him make millions in their joint business careers.

Steve and his team of volunteers are still soliciting gifts in the high six- and seven-figure category. He continues to look at ways to get upfront and specific in each of those major-donor requests. Steve understood this principle and worked it to near perfection. He is very willing to vary the pitch. No conundrums in their campaign!

In your pre-campaign study, you will need your top ten donors to account for one third of your campaign goal. Ask the tough questions upfront. Who are those donors? How well do you know them and can you call them and get a personal appointment in a week or so? Treat each major-donor prospect and suspect as a mini-campaign. Define their hot buttons and invite them to give in their areas of interest and passion. "Dating" your donors is a great way to really get to know them. Clearly define in their individualized proposals what you have determined excites those major donors and causes them to "pound the table" and get excited. Now this all assumes you have those major-donor relationships. If you have not built and enhanced those relationships, you may need to identify that as a potential campaign conundrum. Back up, extend your campaign planning a bit, and build those relationships. Or look at who personally knows those major donors and can cut down on that time frame. Our strategy for major donors is five fold with the five R's: Research, Romance, Request, Recognition, and Recruitment. (See chart on page 66.)

Principle 7
Every Organization Wants Large Capital Dollars from Their Donor File but Few are Willing to Invest the Time and Money Required to Secure Those Gifts and Commitments

The Five R's

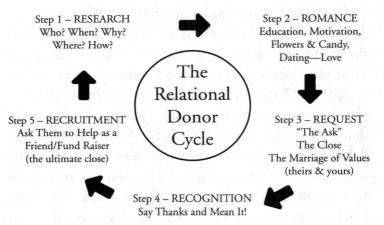

Step 1 – RESEARCH
Who? When? Why?
Where? How?

Step 2 – ROMANCE
Education, Motivation,
Flowers & Candy,
Dating—Love

The
Relational
Donor
Cycle

Step 5 – RECRUITMENT
Ask Them to Help as a
Friend/Fund Raiser
(the ultimate close)

Step 3 – REQUEST
"The Ask"
The Close
The Marriage of Values
(theirs & yours)

Step 4 – RECOGNITION
Say Thanks and Mean It!

Somehow we have lost sight of "high touch" in our high tech society. The most popular method of raising funds is direct mail. It certainly has its strong points, and it can be cost effective and easily performed. You can blanket a large group of people, share a compelling story, and make a credible request for funding. But direct mail is impersonal and rarely builds the depth of relationship needed to target a donor for a six- or seven-figure gift. Imagine the only way to meet and communicate with a potential spouse is by direct mail or email. The relationship can only go so far without personal contact. Chat rooms on the Internet have proven at times to be dishonest as well as dangerous communication. My point is that you will find it very difficult if not impossible to conduct a capital campaign by direct mail, email, or snail mail.

To clarify this point a bit more here are the close and response ratios for the most popular methods of fundraising practiced in the US and Canada.

Methodology	Close Ratio
Direct Mail	1-5%
Telephone	30% (often with lapsed donors)
Group Events	50%, if they know it is a fundraising event, and if the right person invites them to attend (friend raising factor)
Personal Solicitation	75-80%+, if the right person makes the request and the prospective donor has a relationship with the organization or a key player (board, staff, volunteer, CEO, etc.)

Do you want to be successful with your capital campaign? Here is a very simple formula. My friend Alan Duble of the Canaan Group has given this profound advice over the years: See the people. See the people. See the people.

One major donor visit in a capital campaign can produce more gift income than an entire year of direct mail. One well-prepared major-donor prospect can provide the momentum to either catapult a campaign from its beginning (quiet/leadership phase) or provide the final gift to create a fulfillment celebration. Yes, I understand your concern from a time and financial commitment, but getting personally acquainted with your high-capacity donors will make a significant impact on your capital campaign. If you want to be successful with your campaign, invest the time and money to get to know your major-donor prospects and suspects. Want a conundrum-free campaign? Stop sending direct mail only and go see your donors in person.

Principle 8
Major Donors Are Both Customers and Salespeople in the Capital Campaign Process

"Get the brightest and the best committed first." I am not certain of its origin but this is a great concept. You need to start your capital campaign at the top of your donor pyramid, not at the bottom, or you will flame out rather quickly. A bottom-to-top campaign is a conundrum in the making. So you must start at the top and invite your major donors to help you set the pace with their leadership-size gifts.

Remember, a large and unique nation of people made the mass exodus from Egypt; most estimates are around three million, give or take a few thousand. Moses began at the top in Exodus 25, asking for gifts of gold, silver, and bronze, and then moved down throughout the nation. So I have a sneaking suspicion that he and Aaron understood this campaign principle. I believe they were successful because, as they recruited a donor (customer) to give to the tabernacle project, they also recruited those same donors to help them with other donor prospects and suspects. They asked those key donors with the resources to make their commitment first and then invite their friends and traveling companions to join them.

Major donors are both the customer and the sales person in a capital campaign.

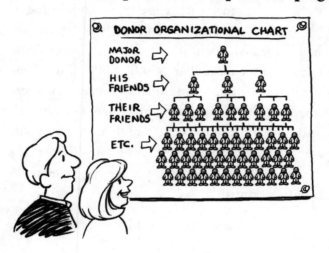

NEWS FLASH! Move forward more than ten thousand years in our cultural and societal development and this is still the way great campaigns are conducted. The number one reason people give is because of who asks. There is a relationship between the asker and the askee. Good news. We are still a relational society and high touch still works. It is sometimes much easier for a major donor to invest dollars in your campaign than time, but you need both. From the salesperson standpoint, think about it. Who do major donors hang around with, vacation with, golf with, live near? The answer is obvious—other major donors. They are people of affluence but are also often people of influence.

We are involved in a campaign now where a major donor flew to another state in his personal plane to invite a very close business friend and investor to match his own

...high touch still works.

million-dollar gift. He said, "I believe I have enough skin in the game to ask my close friend to join me in this campaign." He went on to say that he had helped his friend build equity in his business that had just sold for more than $50,000,000. Can I hear all of you say that the transition from customer to salesperson was made in this campaign? If your major donors invest not just their time, their talent, and their treasure (skin in the game) in your campaign but also invite others to do the same, you are on the way to a productive, potentially conundrum-free campaign.

Campaign Road

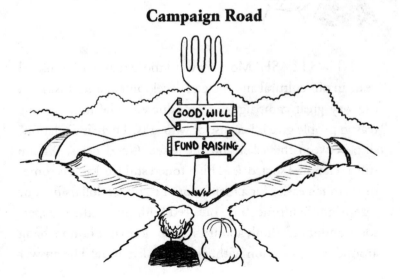

Principle 9
Capital Campaigns Are Comprised of Two Very Different but Equally Significant Parts: The Private Mathematics of the Gift Chart (Fundraising) and the Public Mechanics of Momentum (Good Will)

As the following graphic demonstrates, campaigns often break down into thirds. In a perfect world and in a conundrum-free campaign, your gift chart and giving would show one third of your gifts given by your top ten donors, one third by the next one hundred donors, and the remaining third by the rest of your donor base.

Sources of Gifts in Capital Campaigns

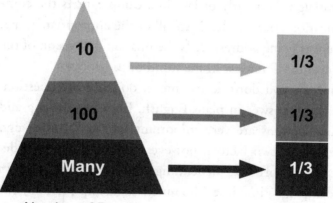

Number of Donors   Proportion of Gifts

Another illustration of this occurred some years ago at a national seminar. A man asked me which is more important in the overall development/advancement campaign process, fundraising or public relations (the generation of good will). Great questions require great—or at least good—answers. In a teaching format I often answer a question first with another question. I believe this helps those asking grasp what the real question is, allowing really deep learning to take place. And many times they end up answering their own question.

which is more important... fundraising or public relations...

So here was my response: "Which is more important to a bird in flight, its right wing or its left wing?" The man immediately complained that I didn't answer his question. But I did answer his question with this further reply: "For the bird, it depends on the wind, the weather, the path of flight (up or down), if the bird is tired, etc." Similar factors can have an impact on a campaign. Is it early or late in a campaign? Is the communication strategy clear? Are all of the appropriate target audiences being addressed? Is the mission and vision of the organization foremost in the mind of the donors?

Just so you don't accuse me of dodging the question, here is my answer in plain English. Both fundraising and public relations are very important for capital campaign success. The two factors, however, will have differing degrees of importance, depending upon where you are in the campaign time line (the quiet/leadership phase or the public phase). Your organization will probably communicate differently to your top one hundred donors than to those who make up the rest of your donor file. The message will remain the same for both fundraising and good will but your methodology will vary. Public relations through personal visits versus indirect contact through mail, email, telephone, and the like provide a foundation for fundraising. Good news is communicated up and down the donor base but bad news (campaign delays, no's on large requests, etc.) are usually communicated up the donor scale by those who have already made large investments.

Communicate with your major donors like investors, not like customers or participants. If you had eggs and bacon this morning for breakfast, here's an analogy for you. The hen was a *participant* in your breakfast but the pig was an *investor*. You must get the right information to the right donor segments to maintain good will in your campaign. This is where outside consulting help is a great investment. After hundreds of successful campaigns we have been there and done that. We know how to help you effectively communicate the right message to the right audience at the right time. Conundrum-free campaigns carefully plan for both fundraising and good will to be emphasized during the shelf life of your capital campaign (two, three, four, or five years).

Principle 10
Your CEO Needs to Be the Number-One Fundraiser and Cheerleader in Your Capital Campaign

A foundation asked us to call a college president and chat about our capital campaign services. In fact, the foundation agreed to underwrite the costs for the pre-campaign study. When I finally reached the president by telephone his voice mail message indicated he was out of the office on donor visits. My next attempt also failed because the president once again had scheduled donor visits. When I later commended him on his performance, he merely stated, "I was just out doing my job." I loved it. Remember? See the people. See the people. See the people. Prior to a campaign this president was out in the field calling on donors, building and enhancing relationships.

When the tough questions are asked, your CEO must provide the answers.

I know that some CEOs, presidents, executive directors, headmasters, and headmistresses do not want to hear it, but they need to be the number-one fundraisers in your organization. And the larger the gift requests, the more they need to be involved. Major-donor profiles often show they don't just *have* money, they *make* money (in some cases, lots of money). And they ask major questions, which is how they got to be major donors. So your major donors, foundation directors, and corporate officers for your capital campaign want answers. They want to sit across from the head of your organization, look into his or her eyes, and discuss vision. Many donors will make their decisions based on those meetings.

When the tough questions are asked, your CEO must provide the answers. So especially if your CEO does not feel adequate in this area, he or she must be trained and led to grow in this area of ministry advancement. Most CEOs must be involved in the four R's of your advancement plan: constituent relations; public relations (branding); student or volunteer recruitment, and fundraising. This will encourage the entire organization and set you on course for a conundrum-free campaign.

Principle 11
The First and Worst Mistake in Any Capital Campaign Is Settling for the Wrong Campaign Leadership. Recruit Wisely.

Even if you have a huge development staff, you will need a large group of volunteers to implement a comprehensive capital campaign. The right team of volunteers will help you open new donor doors, build organizational capacity, and ensure the campaign goal is met. Many a conundrum has developed in a campaign because of ineffective leadership. From campaign chair to committee/team chairs to your committees/teams, recruit capable, faithful, loyal, and committed workers. Provide opportunities for these campaign leaders to take ownership of your campaign. Recruit the brightest and the best volunteers just as you recruit the brightest and the best donors, and then train and empower them to help you succeed.

In the October 26, 2006, *USA Today* sports section there was an article on Wake Forest University. Wake is a small Division I-A university with four thousand students, the second smallest NCAA university of the 119 competing at that level. Listen to this profound statement by their athletic director, Ron Wellman: "Our mission statement is to excel in everything we do because we have the resources to embrace that. We expect to challenge for Atlantic Coast Conference titles and that in turn will make us competitive nationally." The secret to Wake's success? "Hiring good coaches and keeping them," Wellman says. "If you have that in place, it will be reflected in the teams you produce.

Sometimes a team falls short of its coach, but I've never seen a team outperform its coach."[9]

By the same token, it will be difficult to outperform

...the key to our success is our campaign leadership.

the quality of the volunteer leadership dedicated to your campaign effort. Use the Wake Forest model. Recruit wisely and empower them to help you perform your campaign tasks.

I have worked on a campaign that used the services of over one hundred campaign volunteers and one that recruited and trained two hundred volunteers. All of the volunteers in both of these campaigns had a job description and functioned under the able leadership of good advancement staff and very engaged volunteer leadership.

I've mentioned Steve Wilson, the advancement director at Lakeland Christian School, before. He is near fulfillment of phase II of a $16 million capital campaign. Phase III will be a science/technology complex, and they will need to raise an additional $11 million for a total of $27 million. Their largest capital campaign prior was $2.5 million.

"Pat," Steve said, "we have great material, a good plan, excellent training, and mentoring by The Timothy Group. But the key to our success is our campaign leadership. Your Timothy Group campaign manual provided comprehensive job descriptions for our campaign volunteers, even in our pre-campaign study." We lined up a number of key leaders in the study but Steve handpicked his leadership team. "We have recruited committed community leaders and they are winners," Steve said. "They have not failed in their lives and businesses and will not allow our campaign to fail. These people have placed their personal and professional reputations on the line with us, and their names are printed in the campaign material."

Steve also mentioned that this was the first time in their fifty-five-year history that campaign leadership/volunteers actually asked for money themselves. This campaign was very volunteer-driven, not just staff-driven. LCS has used three different volunteer campaign leaders to make financial requests for three separate seven-figure gifts. For Steve, it has been all about recruiting the right leaders and empowering them to not just talk about the campaign but to get active and make it happen. These trained and empowered volunteers have taken ownership with Steve and headmaster Dr. Mike Sligh for the success of this capital campaign.

For more on working with volunteers and choosing the best and the brightest, see chapter 9. (Here's a clue: Think FAT. But don't worry, it's not what it sounds like!)

Principle 12
No Large Ask Should Be a Big Surprise but Asking Too Low Can Be an Insult

However visionary your campaign may be, good research should provide the basis for most of your major-donor requests, which should not be too high and certainly should not be too low. In your research you should be able to identify the amount a major donor or perhaps a foundation may be capable of giving.

The next step is to rate your donors. Begin to identify who has the capacity to give at the levels of your gift chart. If you need one gift at $2,000,000 and one gift at $1,000,000 and two gifts at $500,000, you need to put two or three names of donor prospects and suspects beside each of those categories. Your next campaign move is to make an ask, a credible request for financial participation.

[W]e are using the 'gasp method.'

I have often believed if the depth of relationship is evident between the organization and the major donor, it is very difficult to over ask. To ask too low, however, can be an insult to a high-capacity donor.

In one school campaign some years ago, the campaign committee/team rated a dentist and his wife for a $75,000 request, $25,000 a year for three years. A couple of people involved in the rating process really felt the family had that kind of capacity. Take note of this, their gift to the organization the prior year had been just $2,500. While I tagged along on the visit over lunch, the campaign volunteer, Mel (his real name), shared the case statement/leadership proposal and made the request for support. Mel was a dear friend and long-time patient of the dentist.

When he made the ask for $75,000, the dentist literally gasped. He said to Mel, "That is a good bit more than we were thinking of giving." Mel quickly replied, "Yes, Doc, I understand. But this is also the largest step of faith in the history of the school, and we all need to step up and consider a larger gift if we intend to achieve our goal."

The dentist and his wife gave $100,000 to the campaign, $25,000 over the rated and requested amount.

While the couple may have been a bit surprised they were also not insulted. As we left the restaurant, the dentist asked where the request amount had come from. Before I could answer Mel said, "Doc, we are using the 'gasp method.' If you don't gasp when we ask, we know we asked too low."

No large ask should be a surprise, but asking too low in a capital campaign can be an insult.

When and if the gasp comes, hold your ground and explain the details of the campaign. But more conundrums come from under asking because of the potential for an insult than from over asking. No reason to be shy, no surprises. But emphasize opportunity for donors to be stretched and challenged to give big. You will be surprised by the response at these donor visits. You will be surprised but your major donors shouldn't be.

These twelve principles are critical to your capital campaign success. If you adhere to them during your planning and implementation, you will greatly increase your campaign capacity and be on your way to conundrum-free campaigning. Even if you need to back up and address or re-address some issues, that effort will pay dividends in the long and short run. "Go ugly early" (make the tough decisions), and use these principles as soon as possible in your capital fundraising project.

But how do you then proceed toward a well-orchestrated, conundrum-free capital campaign? By moving through the four phases we will explore in the next four chapters.

- Phase I is a pre-campaign study phase (Timothy Group terminology for a feasibility study), which is an opportunity to develop and test your organizational case for support. You accomplish this with internal and external research and objective input.

- Phase II is a quiet/leadership phase, when you recruit your committee/team chairs and begin to solicit leadership gifts.

- Phase III is a public phase (the actual campaign itself), when your committees/teams, divisions, or teams solicit resources within their affinity groups.

- Phase IV is a donor-maintenance phase, a time to thank your donors and prepare for the next campaign.

Let's get started with phase I.

Note: The 12 principles presented in this chapter were developed throughout my 28 years of personal campaign experience with nearly 300 campaigns, as well as principles discussed in a white paper titled, "What you don't know about Capital Campaigns can hurt you." This paper was written by my friend and long time stewardship officer, Dr. Charlie Phillips, USA Director of The Maclellan Foundation, Inc. in 2005.

4

Phase I: The Pre-Campaign Study Phase

"Is there anyone here who, planning to build a new house, doesn't first sit down and figure the cost so you'll know if you can complete it?"
— Luke 14:28 (The Message)

"Feedback is the breakfast of champions."
— Ken Blanchard

You will pay a price if you cut corners in any of the four campaign phases. But, from my experience, skipping the pre-campaign study phase poses the most risk. Why? Because a study lays a strong foundation with clear directions, without which the whole campaign structure is in jeopardy.

Allow me to build the case for pre-campaign studies—using a couple of analogies along the way—and then see if you agree.

A Journey without Directions

Here's a great story. Yogi Berra was once over two hours late for a speaking engagement while driving with his wife, Carmen. Carmen said, "Yogi, admit it, we are lost!" "Yes, honey, we are lost," Yogi replied, "but we are making great time."

Every male in the history of our world has been lost. No one is faulting we men for getting lost . . . hey, stuff just happens! But we would also rather be lost than stop to ask for directions. Most of us, however, do not need a MapQuest print out to drive to the office, our favorite pizza joint, or our grandmother's house. Those trips have an air of familiarity because we have made them many times before and know our way. We may even know shortcuts. But most of us would not think of taking a trip by automobile to a place we had never been without MapQuest, our trusty *Rand McNally Road Atlas*, or a GPS system like Magellan or TomTom. (Well, at least you ladies would not do that.)

It is no different with a capital campaign journey. For many who have been effectively addressing the needs of an annual/operational fund, the capital campaign is a horse of a different wheelbase. You are embarking on a different kind of journey with bigger goals, multiple campaign committees/teams, and a specific time line.

So why do organizations believe they can run a successful, conundrum-free campaign without research to support their plans and goals, taking off on a long, sometimes difficult journey without clear directions or a road map? I don't get it. Our experience clearly in-

Yes, honey, we are lost," Yogi replied, "but we are making great time."

dicates that, without good planning and clear direction, campaign failure is looming. Like Yogi, you can make good time. But how and when will you get there?

I believe your chances of getting lost in the labyrinth of a capital campaign are significantly increased without a pre-campaign study. Yet some organizations still embark on the next three phases of their capital campaigns without a study.

A Weak Foundation

Here's another analogy. If the foundation of a house is not solid, the house may crumble and collapse. If a study is not conducted and real and felt needs are not addressed, your capital campaign may also crumble. Children learn a song in Sunday school (which I used to sing very loudly) about a wise man who built his house on a rock. When the rains and floods came, his house was okay because its foundation was good. But a foolish man built his house on sand, and when the rains and floods came, well…his house went *down*. All the way down. Washed away. You get the idea. Strong foundations make for strong houses, weak foundations may crumble with pressure and the house is going to go with it.

Many years ago, my sons, Seth and Matt, and I built a dog house for our beagle. It was one of those teachable moments. I asked seven-year-old Seth to sketch out some plans for Lady's dog house with a ruler on a sheet of paper. We live in Michigan where it gets pretty cold, and we built it—using Seth's plans in a very general way—with roofing, insulation, and carpet. In reality Lady was an inside dog and seldom used it over the years, yet nothing was too good for our family member and pet. But would you let your seven-year-old draw up plans for your own house? Of course not. You would be unwise to do so. Yes, you *would* have a plan, but it would be incomplete and certainly insufficient for a new house. Needless to say, we revised Seth's plan a good bit as we went along.

Most foundations in the old days were constructed with cement blocks, and many of the new foundations are poured concrete walls, making them more solid and structurally sound. But regardless of the material used, imagine a house with a weak or broken foundation. Only if there are no storms, earthquakes, tornados, wind, rain, humidity—well, you name it—will that foundation last. Now imagine the foundation of your campaign weakened by conundrums in a capital campaign's volunteer structure, specific time line, and myriads of tasks and meetings.

Here we go. You have been waiting for me to say this with great emphasis, so I will: *Another critical step in a capital campaign is research prior to launching your campaign.* Have successful conundrum-free campaigns been conducted without a pre-campaign study? The obvious answer is yes! But The Timothy Group's informal, perhaps a bit non-empirical research conducted with more than fifteen hundred clients in campaigns in the US, Canada, UK, and New Zealand since 1990, indicates there are at least five unsuccessful campaigns for every successful campaign. And we think one of the reasons is that it is so tough to achieve a successful campaign without a study.

Dwight David Eisenhower, a four-star general and United States president, said, "Plans are nothing. Planning is everything." We have seen many campaigns that were apparently conceived on the back of a napkin at a restaurant or at 11:35 p.m. at the end of a very long board meeting. This makes you wonder what kind of thought went into their "planning." And we have been brought in to repair many campaigns that did not

> *"Plans are nothing. Planning is everything."*

have a pre-campaign study. (It is difficult work, and everyone could have been much more productive if research had been completed in advance.) Here is my perception of what people have tried to do when they realize they have a weak foundation:

They go to the weakest point of the block wall, chip out a bigger opening, and dump in a bag or two of Redi-mix cement (it's $6 a bag at Home Depot). Next they put a garden hose into the opening, turn on the water, and pray. Would you buy a house with a shaky foundation repaired with a bag of cement mix and a garden hose? Redi-mix with water will certainly harden, but would you feel confident that the foundation was reinforced in the right spot? No, neither would I! Weak foundation, weak house. That we understand. It is the same with your campaign strategy. Weak capital campaign foundation, weak capital campaign.

Are there different schools of thought on studies? Absolutely! But please reserve final judgment until you finish reading this chapter. Consulting firms around the country make statements in brochures, on their websites, and in their presentation materials like "a feasibility study is a waste of time and money!" I could not disagree more with that statement, which I believe shows a real lack of understanding when it comes to the ramifications of poor vision and planning. Have I made the case? Then read on.

Know Your Donor

Okay, So What Do We Really Need to Know before Launching a Campaign?

Whew! Great question. In simple terms, you need to identify and rally your human resources (volunteers) and financial resources (new and upgraded dollars).

We live in an information age, and extensive donor information floats around on the Internet. But all that kind of information about donors in the world will not tell you (1) if they know, love, and trust your organization, (2) if they will invest their time, talent, and treasure to help you ac-

This is not rocket science. It is, in fact, all about relationships.

complish your campaign goal, and (3) if the relationships between your organization and your donors are strong enough that they will also help you sell the campaign to their friends.

With a pre-campaign study, we want to identify three major factors to understand the heartbeat, capacity, and capability of the high capacity and a selected list of representative donors in your donor base.

Factor 1: ME (WHO I AM)

You only get to know people by building relationships with them. Understand what makes your donors tick. What are their specific areas of passion? Find out who they really are and how they fit into your campaign plans.

Me!

Factor 2: MY THING (WHAT I DO)

Find out what your donors do for a living. Are they in-dependently wealthy? Do they sit at home and play the stock market? Are they international business people? Are they plumbers? Guess what, all of those people can play a key role in your campaign. Whether they make gifts of cash, donations of in-kind goods and services, or donations of accumulated assets, you want and need them involved in your campaign.

My thing!

Factor 3: MY THINGS (WHAT I HAVE)

Every capital campaign is easier and more effective if you have identified a number of major donors. Dis-cover who is on your major/mega donor radar screen. What do these donors have in the way of hard assets that can be invested in your capital campaign effort?

What can these donors give over and above their current level of giving to your organization?

My things!

The benefits of discovering who your donors are, what they do for a living, and what they have to invest in your campaign are many, and among the reasons I am a strong proponent of the pre-campaign study. These three factors (me, my thing, my things) are just another way of answering the time, talent, and treasure question. You will not only know if you have the human resources (volunteers) and financial resources (dollars) you need to conduct a successful, conundrum-free campaign, you will also form a deeper bond with your donors.

This is not rocket science. It is, in fact, all about relationships. As I mentioned in chapter 3, your pre-campaign study should help you identify organizational strengths but will most certainly help identify weaknesses. Hear me out. Without a study you have no choice but to make a number of major-league assumptions. Do you want to make those assumptions and be wrong? Only in the midst of a campaign, in the real intense heat of battle, do you begin to experience conundrums.

I am not talking about speed bumps; I have seen mountain-size conundrums because organizations just did not recognize the value of gathering research on their donors and spending the time and resources to build or strengthen those relationships. Every donor relationship requires both art and science. The science of donor information management defines giving patterns, frequency of giving, source codes (what stimulates the donor to give), etc. The art of donor relationships is about getting to know the donor, finding out what makes him or her tick. Find out what donors do from 8-5 every day, discover areas of passion, and begin to help lead them toward a major gift opportunity. If you are going to err in a conundrum-free capital campaign, err on the side of the science of the relationship, not on the art. Your pre-campaign research and romance will strengthen and enhance those important donor relationships.

Internal Research

Determine early if you have the internal capacity to conduct a successful capital campaign. Let's ask it a simple way: Are you ready? The donors, dollars, and volunteers may be out there for your organization, but if you are unable to access them, oops, another campaign conundrum.

Your internal research is critical to laying a solid foundation upon which to build $500,000 to $110 million campaigns. Those are the highs and lows of campaigns we have been privileged to service over the years. Here are some of the questions you should ask yourselves:

1. Are you using good, user-friendly donor software that will help you wisely manage the campaign process? (More on that in chapter 7.)
2. Do you have the staff to make it happen? No, I am sorry to report that a comprehensive capital campaign cannot be totally driven by volunteers. You will need staff ownership and participation.
3. Is the leader of your organization ready to step up and present your campaign case to the top 25-100 donor prospects and suspects?
4. Will your board/advisory board step up and give financially? Will your board membership also serve in the campaign structure as fundraisers and friend raisers?
5. Key volunteers making key donor contacts (asking for money) within the framework of the campaign adds instant credibility to your effort. Is there a "campaign attitude" within your internal organization to provide energy, expertise, and passion for this project?

Also ask the questions in the "A" section of the ABC's of capital campaigns below and then consider the points in the "B, C and D" sections. After all this, you'll soon be on your way to a conundrum-free campaign.

The ABC's of Capital Campaigns

A sk the Tough Questions Upfront

1. Does your organization have a well-honed, thoughtful mission statement that is clearly communicated and understood by the board, administrators, faculty, and/or current or potential constituents?
2. Do you have a current strategic plan that evokes the vision of an exciting future for the organization that will benefit every customer and service recipient?
3. Does this strategic plan have an appropriate price tag attached to it?
4. Does your board of trustees give generously to your organization?
5. Is your CEO/president an effective fundraiser?
6. Does your development/advancement office regularly conduct successful annual fund drives?
7. Does your operating budget balance each year?
8. Are the donors, staff, and constituents proud of your organization?
9. Do you have a track record of success and proof of effective stewardship?
10. Can you explain what makes your organization distinctive and worthy of support?

B efore You Move Forward

1. If any of the tough questions got a negative response, you may not be ready.

2. Consider the terrible cost of a failed campaign.
3. Go back to work to correct the issues or items.
4. You can get ready with a good plan.

Campaign for All You Are Worth

1. You are ready if all of the tough questions got a positive response.
2. Conduct your pre-campaign study.
3. Establish a campaign goal that stretches the institution.
4. Establish a board steering committee/team to solicit trustees first.
5. Recognize the importance of the CEO and the director of development in the campaign.
6. Conduct the quiet/leadership phase of the campaign. (Use the 5 R's: Research, Romance, Request, Recognition, and Recruitment.)
7. Invite the full organization family to participate during the public phase of the campaign.
8. Celebrate the victory. Be sure to say thank you!

Do it Again, Only Bigger

1. Don't disband your entire campaign team.
2. If the campaign has been successful, your team and the ministry family may be hungry for more. (David slew the bear before he slew Goliath.)
3. Establish new goals, and do a good job with Recognition (say thanks) and Recruitment (network with their friends) for all donors.

4. Build a strong, ongoing stewardship program (annual, capital, endowment funding).

External Research

Will Rogers said it best: "The common thing about commonsense is it ain't that common." Take a very commonsense approach to your external research. Determine what information you really need to know prior to launching a campaign. Here is my commonsense approach to what you must learn.

1. Are your ministry programs effective and necessary? Is there a duplication of services with some other organization? What makes your outreach unique?
2. Is your case for support strong, understood, and well received by your constituency?
3. Are your mission, vision, and core values understood by your constituency?
4. Do you know the key volunteers who will help you open new and existing doors of opportunity and will populate your divisional campaign committees/teams?
5. Do you know where half to two thirds of your current giving level campaign monies will be given? You know the money is out there but will they give to the campaign at this time?
6. Is your organizational brand, your image, your reputation in your universe (community/constituency) strong and one that will excite donors to help you accomplish your campaign goal?

7. Are you well respected by other agencies in your service area? You do not have to be best friends, but mutual respect among your peers may be an issue as you plan and implement your campaign. Envy and jealousy of your plans and purposes by other organizations will quickly sort themselves out as you conduct external research.

These questions are by no means exhaustive but the answers will give you a good perspective on what those outside of your ministry office think about your organi-

Take a very commonsense approach to your external research.

zation. The reality is somewhat harsh: Your donors vote with their checkbooks. If you cannot answer many of these questions to be certain you have the support of your donors with their time, talent, and treasure, campaign fulfillment is going to be a struggle.

Case Statement

Do you have a document that clearly defines the history, mission, vision, and core values that drive your organization? Oh, I understand your organizational case for support is in someone's mind and heart (your CEO, president, executive director, or administrative team). But is it down on paper or on someone's hard drive? Can it be easily duplicated and shared with any and all of your target audiences? Does it define the human need that drives your organization? Issues like evangelism, discipleship, mercy ministries, education, and specific services to men, women, children, and families must be clearly defined in your case statement. Does this plan have a price tag attached—how much it will cost to accomplish this vision? Case development is a very important part of any campaign, be it annual, capital, or endowment. An informative, compelling, graphically pleasing case statement is another step in planning a conundrum-free campaign.

Questionnaire

A questionnaire is another key component of your pre-campaign study. If you only do a capital campaign every five to ten years, here is your opportunity to ask some questions you have really wanted to ask.

Good empirical research is important to every campaign. Data gathering questions (name, address, phone and cell phone numbers) can be easily answered, but what about getting additional information?

• Discover your donors' religious or church affiliations. Are they Baptists or Buddhists?
• Gather as many email addresses as possible.
• Ask for their age range. This will help identify candidates for your planned giving efforts.
• Find out more about who the donors really are. Are they service recipient alumni or parents of alums? Are they grandparents? Are they related to a staff member?
• Knowing how they originally became donors to your

organization may be helpful for future donor acquisition opportunities.

• Certainly you want to ask if they will give over and above their current level of giving and how much (at least a range of giving).

We also use the study to build a team of volunteers. Ask your donors and close friends if they will step up and become campaign volunteers. Query them about becoming a "fundraiser" or a "friend raiser" because you will need both in your campaign. Our research shows that people often do what you ask them to do. Don't complain you have no volunteers if you have not asked people to participate.

Good empirical research is important to every campaign.

You can also very specifically ask them to help you rate the importance of your case and campaign priorities. Are your fees too high or too low? What other schools, colleges, or ministries (your competition) do they actively support or are in their circles of influence? There is no reason to end your pre-campaign study with questions about your constituents unanswered. Ask good questions and you often get good answers. You will want your case and questionnaire short enough that your constituents can carefully read the case for support document and thoughtfully complete the questionnaire in thirty to forty five minutes or less.

Segmentation Strategy Methods to Obtain Feedback

Segmentation strategy is the process of selecting who will be interviewed for your pre-campaign study and how. You can query donors, key friends, philanthropists, local stewards, service recipient alumni, and foundations in one of four different ways.

1. In person — with top-level donor prospects and suspects
2. By telephone — after you have mailed a case statement and questionnaire
3. By mail — with a BRE (Business Reply Envelope) to help them easily return the completed questionnaire
4. By email — proven to be an effective method for empirical research with certain segments of a donor file

So the $64 million question is this: With what method should you contact each potential donor? Think like Moses and Aaron did in Exodus 25. Everyone participated in their campaign but they started at the top and worked their way down. They began their research and campaign with those who could share gifts of gold, silver, and bronze.

Why would you think you should do it any other way? A $3,000,000 and a $30,000,000 campaign are both big tasks and difficult to achieve without lead gifts from major donors. You will need donors who can give an additional $25 to $100 a month but you also need donors who can contribute $100,000 to more than $1,000,000 over the three to five years of your campaign. Donor prospects and suspects are key. Do not use the study to interview people who have money but no interest. A handful is fine but you will not want to interview all—or mostly all—strangers. People who have already indicated their interest in your organization by their donor track record are those who must be visited in the study. If people do not know your mission and buy into it, the interview, if obtained at all, is liable to be fairly brief and often ends with a very small or no gift indication.

How Else Will You Know?

Once again, a pre-campaign study is a great way to lay the foundation for a conundrum-free campaign. How else will you gather information you need? How will you know what people are thinking and how they will respond to your campaign? How, when asked during an initial visit to a foundation or when you receive a letter, will you be able to say how much money your pre-campaign study indicated you could raise? This is where those in the "no pre-campaign study" camp have a tough time justifying their campaign. I am not sure how I would answer the question without a study. I have been asked the question a number of times. It is, in my humble yet vast experience, a fair question. The foundation, corporation, and/or giving source protects itself by making a giving decision based upon sound fundraising principles.

Plan your work, then work your plan. A well-rounded, comprehensive, pre-campaign study will help your organization make some critical decisions before it goes forward.

For some organizations we even recommend some small

group pre-campaign study informational events, a "major-donor focus group," if you will. Ask those who have the most capacity to help you set the pace early in your campaign to attend. Often during the study interview major donors ask who else you plan to interview as a part of this process. Once again, it is a fair question. But I believe they are really asking who the other major donors are who will help ensure the success of your campaign. You will eliminate that question with your pre-campaign study major-donor focus groups because your major donors will meet other major donors there. You can also announce who else is being invited to attend other focus groups.

The pre-campaign study is a clever and efficient method of conducting research and romance with your major-donor prospects and suspects. Grease the skids for the early gifts to your campaign by sharing your vision with your top ten to one hundred or more donors you know will help carry the day.

Pre-Campaign Study Surprises

After all these years and all these clients, you would think there would be no more surprises in the campaign business. I hope you join me, however, in recognizing the power of God in this universe. The Almighty, who both spoke the universe into existence and is concerned about the sparrow, wants your campaign to be successful. As good as your development, marketing, and communication efforts are, an information gap still exists.

I still discover donors—particularly those with major

capacity—who don't totally understand organizational mission, vision, and core values when they are approached. One of the reasons I am and will always remain a field person is because the best research is conducted while sitting in front of a donor, sharing vision and asking questions. I have actually seen a handful of campaigns begin to take shape during interviews in a pre-campaign study. Conundrums will always be a possibility, but you begin to address one of the worst potential conundrums when a few donors show you they really do have the capacity to fund your vision. Here are a few miracles that God—not the men and women of The Timothy Group—performed in front of our eyes during pre-campaign studies.

> *Plan your work, then work your plan.*

A Big Donor in the Big Apple

A small New York City ministry doing mobile outreach to those in need in the five boroughs employed us to do a pre-campaign study. I spent a day with one of their teams in the Bronx. What a delightful day that was, sharing food, hope, and help with people who desperately needed it. To move forward with their mission, we had recommended a study to help prepare the staff, board, and constituency for a capital campaign. Their annual fund budget the past fiscal year had been $250,000, and they had never done a pre-campaign study or a capital campaign. Their vision and case statement defined a campaign need of $2,600,000, over ten times the size of the annual fund.

My colleague at The Timothy Group, Kent, and I jumped on the subway trains and conducted personal interviews all over New York City and in New Jersey. I interviewed one man who had contributed $2,500 to the ministry's annual fund the previous year. We get very specific in our interviews, and I asked him what he believed he might be able to contribute over the next three years over and above his current level of giving if the campaign were launched. As I often do, I turned around the study questionnaire so he could see the dollar amount categories.

Something interesting happened on the seventeenth floor of that Manhattan office building. The man checked the $500,000 box and handed it back to me. I thanked him and was ready to move on to the next question when he asked for the questionnaire back. He crossed out the $500,000 box and checked the $1,000,000 box.

"Inquiring minds want to know," and I was one of those inquiring minds. I said, "Paul, I am very thankful for your gift indication, but help me understand. You are going from $2,500 annually to $333,000? Why?" His reply? "This is the largest need in the history of a ministry I know and love, and I now have the capacity to give at that level."

He went on to say that his company had just been sold for nearly a billion dollars and he was in an equity/ownership position. The interview was in early August, and I knew the ministry was on a tight time frame and had some start-up campaign costs/needs. So I asked him how soon he could begin giving, and he said he could give $500,000 by calendar year end. You make the call. Is there good rationale to conduct a pre-campaign study prior to launching your capital campaign? I believe there is. But please read on.

What Would You Do with a Million-Dollar Gift?

A ministry's brand new donor asked a very interesting question during our pre-campaign study interview. He had read the case statement, and we were well into the questionnaire when he said, "Let's get to the bottom line. What would your organization do with a million-dollar gift?" He went on to ask how soon the organization would break ground, what the building might look like, etc.

I rarely do this, but on this interview a ministry representative had joined me for the pre-campaign study call. Here is why I am glad the ministry representative was along. The next question the donor asked was, "What would the ministry do with a $5,000,000 gift?" The family ended up giving a total of $8,000,000 to the campaign.

In this pre-campaign interview, the donor was really asking if there was enough vision in the campaign and the organization to meet his capacity as a major donor. Remember, one of the twelve capital campaign principles is that the real benefit of a capital campaign case for support is that it tests the state of your case. Another principle is that all stewardship dollars flow on trust but big capital dollars rise to the height of organizational vision. In essence, this major donor was testing the case for support and testing the height of the organizational vision. Questions like these will often be asked in a pre-campaign study interview and are another reason we think the research is beneficial. Major donors ask major questions, and the study is an excellent format to receive and answer those questions.

"I Can't Give a Gift of Cash but I Want to Help"

The purpose of a pre-campaign study is to identify gifts of cash; appreciated, planned and deferred gifts; and in-kind gifts. When donors in the study interviews indicate they love your case for support, believe in your ministry, and want to help but cannot give a cash gift, what do you do? You continue your research by asking, "How could you help us with a non-cash gift of value?"

> ...*the donor was really asking if there was enough vision ... to meet his capacity as a major donor.*

We had just that conversation with a builder a few months ago. We had clearly defined our capital needs and construction plan. The first step was to build a maintenance building on the other side of campus, with a price tag of $585,000. The builder and donor (parent of an existing student) was asset-rich but cash-flow poor. He agreed to build the building as his gift to the campaign.

A couple of weeks ago I saw almost all the blocks for that building in place, and the organization's 25,000 square foot building is well underway. This conversation was a part of the pre-campaign study, and it resulted in a pure-donation, non-cash gift with a $585,000 value. Now the organization does not have to raise cash for this need.

In another study in Alaska, the organization felt a donor had the capacity to give a seven-figure gift because of his long-term knowledge of the organization and previous giving history. The donor indicated during the study, however, that he and his wife could only consider a non-cash gift. They contributed a duplex and two large wooded lots in two different subdivisions. The appraised value of the three pieces of donated property? You guessed it! One million dollars and some change. Once again, the value of the pre-campaign study is finding out what can be given prior to the actual campaign. Without the study, you just won't know.

$10,000 Donor Gets Interested and Excited

In every pre-campaign study, we ask the client to provide a profile for each of the donors they want us to visit in the personal interview process. I saved this typewritten donor prospect introduction which was made by a school's director of development. I think you will find it interesting.

What I know of (name of donor) is that he just sold a local theme park (name of park) and netted $20 million. That apparently is a portion of his money. He seems very private and hard to reach. Our CEO told me he would take me to lunch if I even got him to answer the phone. After scheduling the appointment, I think my CEO should buy me dinner. He has grandchildren at our institution and is hopeful we will accept another special needs grandchild for the coming year.

His family has offered to pay all costs associated with this special needs program. He gives $10,000 annually to our institution and I would not know (name of donor) if he walked in my office right now.

In the very cordial, one-hour interview I subsequently had with this donor, he shared a passion for both an annual operating/program-driven funding need as well as interest in seeing a major capital campaign launched. When we got to the range of giving/money section of the questionnaire, he would not indicate a specific amount. But he did make this statement:

"As a family we would like to see this educational program added to the school, and we are excited about the potential three-phased capital campaign." (A precampaign study should position campaigns in phases.) He went on to say, "If those two projects have the potential of becoming a reality, we have the capacity to contribute several million dollars." When I thanked him for his keen interest and then asked him what "several million dollars" meant, he told me in the $3-$5 million range.

This donor shared how busy and profitable their various companies were, and I became convinced this was a really high-capacity donor. I went back to the school and asked the CEO and director of development how fast they could get out and introduce themselves to this donor. Remember, the director of development said he would not know this donor if he walked into his office!

They got to know this donor and his family, who have since generously invested their time, talent, and treasure in the school. They have helped access their contacts in a variety of businesses and corporations to help in the capital project in particular. And, oh, by the way, to date the family has contributed $4,500,000 toward the school's academic and capital projects.

How will you lay a solid foundation for a conundrum-free capital campaign if you do not ask questions and invite people to step up as never before to invest in your organization? How will you know who will serve on your campaign committees/teams and open new doors to foundations, corporations, philanthropists, and new giving sources? You need donor research, and certainly some of it can come from scientific, hard-asset research by one of the search organizations (Target America, Wealth Engine, Blackbaud, etc.). But you will never find the "millionaire next door" unless you sit down and have a discussion over a case statement and a questionnaire. As high tech as we have become in our society, organizations still need to be high touch with their donor base.

As high tech as we have become in our society, organizations still need to be high touch with their donor base.

John Humphrey, a partner at the high-tech software company Pariveda Solutions in Dallas, told me that 67 percent of all business communication in the world is non-verbal. High-tech communication will not achieve the goal you desire in your donor research. A pre-campaign study allows you to be high touch in defining your current services and the need to move forward with a capital campaign to fund new programs, purchase new property, and add new personnel (the 3 P's of capital campaigns).

Please understand, I firmly believe Psalm 127:1 (NLT): "Unless the LORD builds a house, the work of the builders is wasted." But I also firmly believe conundrum-free campaigns begin with good research.

The success stories I just shared with you may have become a reality without a study, but I don't think so. So I ask you to carefully and prayerfully consider all options before launching a campaign to give your organization a fair opportunity for a conundrum-free campaign. Plan your work, then work your plan. Proverbs 29:18 (KJV) says, "Where there is no vision, the people perish." A study gives you that additional opportunity with donors to test your organizational/campaign vision. It allows you to raise the flag and see who salutes. As good as you think your plan may be, if your donor base does not show approval of your plan in a study you cannot and will not be successful.

Will you discover surprises in your pre-campaign study? Absolutely! Will you be surprised by some of the organizational weaknesses and strengths you discover? Without a doubt. But if your case for support finds favor, the surprises will be similar to the success stories in this chapter. It's your road map to a successful, conundrum-free campaign. Or as business consultant Basil S. Walsh writes, "An intelligent plan is the first step to success. The man who plans knows where he is going, knows what progress he is making, and has a pretty good idea of when he will arrive."

Want a conundrum-free campaign? The cures for campaign conundrums are often discovered when an organization conducts a comprehensive pre-campaign study upfront. A study will help you establish benchmarks, chart the right course, and move forward with a conundrum-free campaign.

5

Phase II:
The Quiet/Leadership Phase

*"Example is not the main thing in
influencing others. It is the only thing."*
— Albert Schweitzer

Leaders lead, and that very simple but profound concept
can make or break your capital campaign. Conundrum-
free campaigns are blessed with great teams of leaders who
have been recruited, trained, educated, and solicited. But
if you find no one is following them, they probably aren't
really leading.

Now is your opportunity to solidify your leaders' involvement early in your capital campaign. Those leaders
among you with the capacity to invest their time, their
talent, and their treasure need to step up and help you

establish the way forward. That's why a well-orchestrated, carefully conducted quiet/leadership phase of a campaign is also foundational to your success and will take you well down the road toward a conundrum-free effort.

Communicate the results of your pre-campaign study with potential leaders and begin this new phase with confidence. Recruit the brightest and the best and empower them. Here are some key concepts and ideas to help you plan and implement the quiet/leadership phase of your capital campaign.

Start with the Information from Your Pre-Campaign Study

Another benefit of a pre-campaign study is that you can roll the momentum from your study right into the quiet/leadership phase of your campaign. You have already queried the leadership families in your constituency. You have taken their temperature and you know if they are hot, cold, or just lukewarm about your ministry and this particular capital project. As you have read a time or two now, conundrum-free capital campaign success is dependent upon the organization's readiness to conduct the campaign. Your organization must already be successful, have a storied history if possible, and more. If it was well done, your pre-campaign study has told you if you have:

Recruit the brightest and the best and empower them.

1. A positive image. People know, love, and respect your organization.
2. Backing for your case for support. People are ready to give and help you solicit others.
3. Real acceptance of your capital wants and needs list. People get it.
4. Available influential and interested volunteer leadership who are ready to step forward.
5. An attainable goal. It's big and stretches you, but you believe you can reach it with a good plan, great leadership, and lots of hard work.
6. The right timing to launch and fulfill your campaign. Remember, the only difference between a home run and a long foul ball is *timing*.
7. A strong, committed CEO, administration, and staff leadership. Without this you will be attempting to push warm wiggly spaghetti uphill. You get the picture.
8. Professional, experienced, and appropriate financial sources. Get help to be successful if you need it. Sometimes you have to spend money to raise money.

You also need to consider these five additional factors from your pre-campaign study that will influence the size and fulfillment of your campaign goal.

1. The projections/ratings for the top donor prospects and suspects from your current constituency.
2. The responses you got from the top donor prospects and suspects from your current constituency.
3. The results of exploratory meetings/solicitation visits

with top prospects and suspects who are *not* a part of your current constituency.

4. The advance commitments you received. Who signed a letter of intent or a commit card or wrote you a check? (Now we are going from "good idea, good goal" to reality.)

5. The state of the local philanthropic/stewardship climate. Is the economy good and on the rebound or in the depths of despair?

How you handle and plan around these factors will determine the success of your quiet/leadership phase.

Moving into the Quiet/Leadership Phase

Your pre-campaign study gave birth to a viable and realistic fundraising campaign. You developed a case for support, you queried your constituency, and you compiled and processed empirical research. You asked specific questions about passion for your project. You asked key donor prospects and suspects how much they would contribute and if they are open to serving as volunteers. Whew! That birthing process was hard work. Now comes the next phase of campaign life.

The early days in the quiet/leadership phase are very important to build a firm foundation and lay the groundwork for a conundrum-free campaign. You can clearly see the campaign taking shape from day one and begin putting arms and legs on your campaign vision. Without a plan you will not pull together the people and priorities you need in this critical phase. The campaign will lose momentum and have the potential to underachieve or die. So please plan to dot every "i" and cross every "t" in this phase.

Oh, and as you begin this phase, don't forget to consider additional discoveries since the pre-campaign study. Who else have you identified and what else did they say they would do to help? Case in point, in one pre-campaign study a donor who was giving $25,000 annually indicated a likely gift of $200,000 if a campaign were launched. When we visited the donor very early in the quiet/leadership phase, we asked for and received a commitment for $300,000. One month later the donor increased that gift commitment to $600,000. Five months later, it was increased to $300,000 a year for four years. Go ahead, do the math. That comes to $1,200,000. I would say that is a determining factor discovered after the pre-campaign study.

Leadership Recruitment

A guiding principle from chapter 3 is recruiting the absolute best volunteers. Recruiting your campaign chair and committee/team chairs is an important part of the quiet/leadership phase. A campaign will rise and fall upon the selection of these very special volunteers, so choose and recruit wisely. Recruit a campaign chairperson or chairpersons—preferably a couple—who will invest time, talent, and treasure in helping your campaign succeed. Select them first and invite them to help you build a team around them. Your campaign chairs will know others who will serve with you in this effort. For a conundrum-free campaign, ask these questions about potential chair candidates:

1. Are they recognized as outstanding citizens, well known and respected?
2. Are they actively involved in their business or profession? Do they occupy a significant leadership position in their own business or professional fields?
3. Do they have flexibility and "give" in their schedules so they can make scheduled and, occasionally, unscheduled meetings?
4. Do they understand your organization and are they willing to invest time to learn even more?
5. Are they able to make good, upfront public presentations and are they able to chair meetings effectively and efficiently?
6. Are they well liked by your team? Do they get positive responses from the campaign committee/team, from your staff, and from donors and the community?
7. Are they willing to make significant and/or sacrificial financial commitments to the campaign?
8. Do they possess personal and business characteristics that complement your organization?
9. Are they capable of delegating well and able to hold committee/team people and staff accountable for assigned tasks?
10. Do they have office staff/administrative assistants capable of handling the extra details inherent to the position of chairperson?
11. Do they have highly visible identities with any other

non-profit organizations?

12. Are they willing to prioritize the campaign duties in all aspects of their personal and professional lives?

13. Do they appear to be in good health and have sufficient energy levels to sustain this effort?

14. Are they team players? Will they be "player coaches" by seeing the end objective and entrusting assigned details to staff and volunteers?

15. Are they positive people and able to encourage those in work well done?

16. Are they on board with working on planned schedules and able to meet key deadlines?

17. Do they love and respect your CEO, and will they work well on a team?

18. Are you convinced they will work hard and lend more than their names to the campaign?

19. Are they current members of your existing governing board?

This is certainly not an exhaustive list and may not be exactly the right list for your conundrum-free campaign. But these kinds of questions will get you well down the road in recruiting the right campaign chairpersons. This chapter began with the concept that leaders lead. Nowhere is this concept more critical than the selection of the right chairpersons to lead your campaign. As you can see in the following chart, careful and prayerful consideration needs to go into this selection. Start at the top and work down. A great campaign chair will help you select and recruit the right campaign committee/team chairs. He or she will also

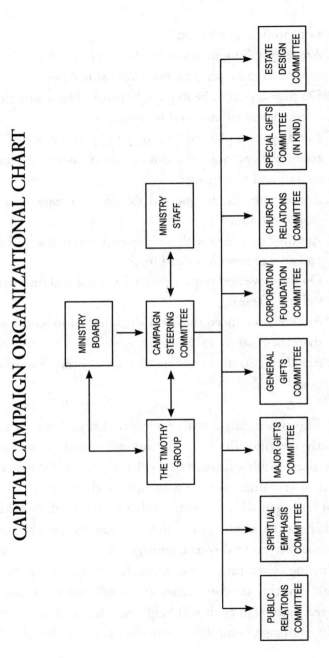

CAPITAL CAMPAIGN ORGANIZATIONAL CHART

help you meld your staff and volunteers into a productive campaign team.

Volunteers Apply Within

A number of years ago, a board member in Canada asked some questions after my presentation on campaign structure. I had just asked the entire group to serve somewhere in the campaign structure and to invest eight to ten hours a month when he asked, "So do we get paid to invest this extra time? How are we compensated for making this campaign a success?"

In all the years of working with so many nonprofits, we have never seen board members compensated for their services. So as you can imagine, I was a bit taken aback. I told him our expectation was for him to do this as a volunteer, and then he indicated he would probably resign. It was all I could do to hold my tongue and not say, "Hey, your resignation would be most welcome." Unfortunately, he did not understand the job description and performance expectations of a typical board member.

Most capital campaigns will use anywhere from twenty five to one hundred volunteers over the course of twelve to twenty four months of solicitation. The quiet/leadership phase is a great time to recruit the right volunteers. I have believed for years—and the conviction only grows on me—that volunteers do what we inspect, not what we expect. Do not even think about recruiting volunteers in your quiet/leadership phase without giving them job descriptions. Know what you want and need for them to accomplish and who will hold them accountable for the tasks you expect them to perform.

Steve Wilson, as the chief development officer at Lakeland Christian School in Florida, is conducting a three-phase campaign to raise $27 million. He shared with me by telephone only two days ago that two of his volunteers had raised the first $500,000 of a new capital project initiative. Yes, you heard it right. Two volunteers, with no staff people on the visit with them, asked for two gifts of $250,000 each . . . and got them. Remember, the number one reason people give is because of who asks. The core value behind using volunteers is that people give to people. Very few campaigns are successful without the effective use of volunteers.

There are three kinds of volunteers in this world: shirkers, jerkers, and workers. You know where I am going. If you have worked with volunteers, you have met all

Shirkers

three flavors just as I have. Shirkers never find the time to volunteer for anything; somehow you are always third or fourth on their priority list. They politely ask you to call back next time you need some volunteer assistance, but you know and they know it will never happen. Again you make the call, but always get a polite, contrite "No."

Jerkers, on the other hand, almost always volunteer and start off with a great blast of energy and enthusiasm (I like to call it a jerk; it's not personal, it's just that quick blast off), followed fairly quickly by their inability to make campaign meetings and "I'm sorry but I have been called out of town" or some other legitimate reason or excuse why they cannot help you. They start out fast but quickly fade.

Jerkers

The final flavor of volunteer is a worker, a real live "show up when you need them" worker. They work hard and will help you whenever and wherever you need them. These are the people you want to recruit to fill out your capital campaign committees/teams. Steve Wilson says these are the volunteers who will make the "ask" while you are off training another volunteer or two so they can accomplish yet another task. I think it was the old knight at the end of

Workers

an Indiana Jones movie who made these two statements to groups seeking the Holy Grail. "He chose wisely" and, to the other group just before they were destroyed, "He chose poorly." When it comes to choosing volunteers, choose wisely!

Campaign Committee/Team/ Division Structure

There is absolutely nothing magical or mystical about the number of campaign committees/teams. Having too many committees/teams may become cumbersome, and having too few committees/teams often does not allow effective distribution of the workload. We have conducted conundrum-free campaigns with ten committees/teams, and we have been successful in other campaigns with just four.

Ergonomics is the study of fit; it's an engineering and design term. Make the number of your capital campaign committees/teams "ergonomically sound." In other words, make it fit your need and organizational capacity. Don't plan to use one hundred volunteers in your campaign if you have only thirty volunteers. Why attempt to have ten committees/teams when five will get what you need to be successful? Once again (I am not sure I can say this enough), populate your campaign committees/teams with leaders who will work hard and honor your campaign calendar and time line. The following campaign structure has worked all over the world with small and very large capital campaigns.

> *Make the number of your capital campaign committees/teams "ergonomically sound."*

30-Second Job Descriptions

If I can't give a concise job description in thirty seconds or less, then shame on me. Please allow me to provide one for each potential campaign committee/team. You'll find more complete job descriptions for each of these committees/teams later in the book.

Major/Lead Gifts: This trained and motivated committee/team will make personal visits to your top 25-200 donor prospects and suspects; often identify sources for one half to two thirds of your campaign goal (think Exodus 25:2-3—first asking those with gifts of gold, silver, and bronze); and identify a donor of affluence and influence early on as a champion of your campaign.

Spiritual Emphasis/Prayer and Praise: Psalm 127:1 (NLT) says, "Unless the Lord builds a house, the work of the builders is useless. Unless the Lord protects a city, guarding it with sentries will do no good." This committee/team will pray for your donors, asking God to open their minds, hearts, and checkbooks. They are empowered to share prayer requests and encourage your entire organization to pray earnestly for God's blessing on the campaign and the conundrums that may surface.

Communications/Public Relations/Brand: This talented group of volunteers is most often staff- and consultant-led. They will help develop your capital campaign theme, logo, brochure, collateral material, and the fundraising tools—DVD's, recruitment brochures, etc.—you will need to succeed. They are almost always the very first campaign committee/team recruited, trained, and empowered. They will help you establish the look, tone, and quality of your campaign material.

Foundation Gifts: Foundations do not give money to proposals, they give to people. This committee/team will be dedicated to reaching out to those unique funding sources for research and romance. Only then can you make a credible request for funds with a better-than-average opportunity for success. This committee/team may be able to solicit foundations on a local, regional, and national basis.

Corporation/Business: This committee/team is comprised of a group of business/corporation types who can help you open the door to corporation and business philanthropic dollars. Though each contact will have some similarities, this committee/team will create tailored request presentations because these potential donors respond to *personal*—and not necessarily to *fancy*—proposals.

Church Partnerships: This committee/team will help expand your capacity in the local/regional/national church marketplace. Churches can be difficult places to raise money but great places to educate and recruit volunteers. This committee/team will help you prepare a unique presentation for each church represented in your constituency. The personal presentation to the mission/deacons/elder board is to invite them to partner with your organization in four distinct ways. (More on that in the next chapter.)

General Gifts: This committee/team will help you determine ways to share the specific needs of the capital campaign with your entire constituency without campaign gifts negatively impacting your annual/operational fund. Those donors who give $25.00 to $100.00 monthly or any amount annually need to be invited to participate financially in the capital campaign. The methodology used here is often direct mail, large and small group events, and wise use of the telephone. Remember, in every donor file is a handful of the "millionaire next door" types.

Alumni: This committee/team will educate, motivate, and solicit your organization's alumni. For obvious reasons, this committee/team is populated by your alums. Often this committee/team organizes and implements an "alumni roll call." It is all about renewing relationships with alumni and making a personal request for their investment in your campaign. The goal is not just fundraising but is—perhaps even more important—also friend raising.

Estate Design/Planned Giving: This committee/team will educate and solicit those who can share gifts of accumulated assets. Often these tax-impacted gifts are actually made in the future, depending on the planned-giving vehicle used. This committee/team is comprised of a financial planner, a bank trust officer, and an attorney. With $11 to $46 trillion changing hands from one generation to the next in the next eight to ten years,[10] the opportunity is obvious. A capital campaign is a great way to organize this critical component of your comprehensive stewardship strategy.

Gifts in Kind/Special Gifts: If your campaign involves brick and mortar, this is an important committee/team. Contractors, sub-contractors, vendors, or suppliers can often make non-cash gifts more easily than they can write a check for your campaign. This committee/team is comprised of those with experience in the building and trades to help you solicit non-cash gifts for your building or program expansion.

By spreading the division of labor among a number of committees/teams or divisions and committed volunteers, you begin to ensure a broad-based effort and create a platform for a conundrum-free campaign.

Capital Campaign Fundraising Tools

Another key component of your quiet/leadership phase is to begin—and I emphasize the word *begin*—to develop your capital campaign fundraising tools. A fundraising tool is a device that will help you share your campaign story and ask for a gift.

Your first fundraising tool is a leadership proposal/partnership document that is nothing more than an expanded case statement. This document can be personalized and can include a specific dollar request. Trust me, this really should be your very first fundraising tool. It can be tweaked and changed to fit the specific needs of a major donor. By fine-tuning this document throughout the course of your quiet/leadership phase solicitation period you will essentially produce the copy for your brochure. We often do not produce a brochure until we go public with the capital campaign. Just as you use a hammer instead of a screwdriver or pliers to drive a nail, you need to use the correct fundraising tool at the right time in the campaign process. Once again, campaign counsel should be able to help you define the plan and time line for developing your campaign tools.

Your first fundraising tool is a leadership proposal

Early on, begin to develop your campaign theme, campaign logo, the masthead for your campaign newsletter, and your campaign letterhead design. You may also want to develop a fundraising tool like a campaign CD or DVD because "a picture paints a thousand words." You will want to begin—only *begin*—your campaign brochure. Don't rush this process. After all, full-color brochures do not raise money, people raise money. I see a number of expensive full-color brochures printed so early in the campaign process that they become outdated too soon. I am serious. A handful of organizations that have ignored our recommended time lines have tossed as many as seventy-five hundred brochures in the dumpster. Remember former UCLA basketball coach John Wooden's wise admonition, "Be quick, but don't hurry."

Start with Communication

The transition from the pre-campaign study phase to the quiet/leadership phase begins with communication with your constituency. Think of the communication strategy from your pre-campaign study in reverse. Announce the results of your study to one segment in person, another segment by telephone, another by mail, and perhaps even a final group of donors by email. While you will communicate with all segments, you will specifically concentrate in this quiet/leadership phase on your board of trustees, administration, key staff, and the donors who participated in the study and have high capacity (five-, six-, and seven-figure gifts).

> *"Be quick, but don't hurry."*

Start with your key, high-capacity donors. After all, bigger dollars add up faster. Remember again that the first gifts Moses and Aaron sought for the tabernacle project in

Exodus 25:2-3 were gifts of gold, silver, and bronze. Go and do thou likewise. It's a great strategy for success. Start at the top and work down.

Second, visit your board members. They may not have huge dollars to invest but the organizational and emotional energy their 100 percent participation can invest in your campaign is truly "priceless."

Next, make personal visits to those donor prospects and suspects whose names surfaced in your pre-campaign study. Rate and rank those donors based upon their knowledge of you and your knowledge of them.

- "A" donors know you and you know them. They may not have been donors in the past but they know your organization and it has credibility with them.
- "B" donors have one-way relationships with your organization. You know them but they do not know you. Or they know a good bit about you but you do not know them. Use these one-way relationships to find good information for a personal visit, and begin to turn them into "A" donor contacts.
- "C" donors are people you do not know personally and they do not know your organization in a personal way. They may currently be small-dollar donors but have the capacity to give much more. Use your quiet/leadership phase to begin to make those romance visits to find levels of opportunity to connect. Discover donor hot buttons for giving and begin to develop those areas of interest.

One final word about those early personal solicitation visits. Please, *please* do not miss this. Rate every donor you will call on in the quiet/leadership phase of your campaign. Am I saying you should ask for specific dollars/pounds/loonies/Euros (you name the form of currency!)? This is exactly what I am saying. If you are not specific and "gra-

Rate every donor you will call on...

ciously aggressive" with financial requests to your key donors, they may have a tendency to "tip God and tip your organization" in this process. If you do not challenge these key donor groups to step up and consider a generous, priority stewardship commitment, they are likely to give well below their potential.

Make bold calls on your gold, silver, and bronze potential donors first, including your board and staff. By involving your board and staff first you can then challenge your major-donor prospects and suspects to join them in raising money to underwrite your campaign.

Transition from the Quiet/Leadership Phase to the Public Phase

How long does it take to conduct an effective quiet/leadership phase and make the transition to the public phase of the campaign? For us, it has taken anywhere from two weeks to eighteen months. Seriously, those are real time frames. In a $6 million campaign we were conducting, in the second week of the quiet/leadership phase we called on a donor and made a $1 million request. The donor thanked us for the request and indicated the family could do more. So I came back and asked the donor to consider a $3 million match (one half of the campaign total) and let him know we would attempt to match his gift. He said they could do it all. Game, set, match—the quiet/leadership phase came to a screeching halt with a successful conclusion in just two weeks.

Now, as you might well imagine, we encouraged the client to increase the campaign goal as it is usually not healthy for one donor to take on an entire campaign goal. But a capital campaign is an excellent time in your stewardship program to upgrade existing donors (as in the case of our $6 million friend) and to add new donors. If we had concluded the campaign with one gift, neither of those goals could have been accomplished. The client immediately began to discuss the need to expand the scope of the campaign and raise dollars for scholarships and faculty endowment.

A more usual length of time is four to eight months. Some campaigns are a bit longer and some, as we mentioned, can be a bit shorter. A number of factors make the difference. If you need to visit one hundred or more major-donor prospects and suspects, that will take more time and a very coordinated effort. Do not shortchange your campaign by rushing the quiet/leadership phase. Take the time you need to solicit all of your major-donor prospects and suspects. Take the time to develop a great campaign theme and logo and create good material. I am encouraging you to carefully plan your work, then work your plan. Every campaign takes on a personality of its own. Your conundrum-free capital campaign begins with a good calendar and time line for each phase.

Show Me the Money

Another major indicator that you are ready to make the transition from the quiet/leadership phase to the public phase is dollars and cents. Cash and commitments will help you determine the right time to make the transition. It is very likely you already have the capacity to raise one half to two thirds of your total campaign goal in your quiet/ leadership phase. Regardless of the size of your campaign goal, if you can raise one half or more of your total in the quiet/leadership phase, you can enter the public phase of your campaign with momentum.

This is the time for your staff and campaign volunteers to implement your plan and raise significant dollars. Show off the money in cash—one- and three-year commitments for your campaign—and you will turn all of your naysayers into believers. You will also convince your target audiences—donors, alumni, parents, grandparents, area philanthropists, foundations, corporations, and businesses—that you have the capacity to fulfill your campaign goal. By becoming public in your media sources (print, electronic, and on websites), you will also convince the community that you have the capacity to fulfill the goals of your campaign. Be smart, be diligent,

Cash and commitments will help you determine the right time to make the transition.

and don't be shy in asking your donors to show you their money.

In summary, identify leaders, train and empower them, and encourage them to help lead you from the starting blocks well into the public phase of your campaign. Don't take any shortcuts. If anything, extend your time line to ensure a successful, conundrum-free capital campaign. Raise one half, two thirds, or even three fourths of your campaign goal during the quiet/leadership phase and you will be ready to move your campaign to the next level: a broad-based, successful, and public capital effort.

6

Phase III: The Public Phase

"A journey of a thousand miles must
begin with a single step." — Lao Tzu

The public phase of your campaign is when you actually conduct the full campaign. You have conducted your
study, and all the results said, "Go for it! Move ahead with
your capital campaign!" You recruited key volunteers who
helped you implement a well-rounded, comprehensive
quiet/leadership phase. Now you are ready to launch the
public phase of your conundrum-free capital campaign.
But what exactly does that mean?

The quiet/leadership phase was low key and under the
radar. You were working with a fairly small number of volunteers and donors. Two to four committees/teams were
active. Now you are ready to let the whole world know

your organization is conducting a capital campaign. Six to ten committees/teams are now going to campaign together. You will build a campaign team of thirty-five to more than fifty volunteers. (Some campaigns have used one hundred or more volunteers.)

You invested time and money in your pre-campaign study and quiet/leadership phases so the momentum would carry you into the public phase of the campaign. Now the campaign has human resources (volunteers and staff) and financial resources (money and commitments). Be ready, for once you publicly launch the campaign, it's out there for everyone to see.

My dear friend and long-time Timothy Group partner, Dr. Howard Nourse, says it like this: "You can't put the genie back in the bottle." Once it's out, it's out! There are no do-overs so your conundrum-free capital campaign has to get it right the first time. You have already worked through two phases with a lot of activity and momentum prior to your public launch. So ready, set, launch!

It's conundrum-free capital campaign time, but before we get started, let's look at this with another couple of analogies.

Think Politics

Every four years in America we have a presidential election. I am over fifty, and I can remember when the campaigning didn't really begin in earnest until after the political conventions the summer before the November election.

Can we all say together, "Boy, has that changed!" I think I can safely say we are now almost never out of a presidential campaign. People declare themselves candidates either formally or informally as early as two years before we can vote them in. Running a successful political campaign takes resources (human and financial). Let's be honest. "Bodies and bucks" are absolute requirements for a good political campaign.

Guess what? It's the same with your capital campaign. You need people to invest their time, talent, and treasure for your effort to be successful. You need to share your message and convince people that

> *"Bodies and bucks" are absolute requirements for a good political campaign.*

your need for a campaign is legit. The right numbers of people (bodies), doing the right things at the right time, bringing in the right amount of cash and commitments (bucks), makes for a conundrum-free, successful capital campaign.

A political campaign needs a number of committees/teams, accomplishing a variety of tasks toward the unified goal of getting their candidate elected. They will raise thousands and, in many instances, millions of dollars to invest in achieving their goal. Your capital campaign will employ a similar strategy: six to ten committees/teams all unified with one campaign agenda, to raise or exceed your stated dollar goal. I am amazed how similar a political campaign is to a capital campaign.

Obviously, your capital campaign will not have spin

doctors, negative advertisements, and the like. But you will use a public relations and communications committee/team to help you clearly define your message. What does this campaign want and need to say about your organization? Why is it important that you raise these dollars? What exactly will the campaign dollars help you do that you cannot do now?

Once again I remind you of the importance of creating a capital campaign that addresses more than just bricks and mortar. Plan to include all three P's (program, personnel, and property) of organization advancement. These are often the hot buttons for your donor base/constituents. Political campaigns are almost never about just one issue, but are about the economy, foreign policy, domestic policy, the environment, and health care, to name a few. Just like in a political campaign, ask yourself, who are the target audiences you need to inform, inspire, and invite to help with a financial contribution?

Share your uniqueness...

Those political campaigns need money to be successful, and so does your organization. Speak clearly, honestly, and passionately to your donors and invite them to be a part of your capital campaign. Share your uniqueness, what makes your organization stand out or stand above the other organizations. I can assure you that, in a crowded field of early Democrat and Republican presidential hopefuls, each are trying desperately to define their unique abilities and perspectives on the issues.

Think political as you get ready to build a campaign

team and then campaign (hopefully conundrum-free) for all you are worth until you reach your goal. It's exactly the same for your capital campaign as for a political campaign. Think about the ole ABC's—Always Be Campaigning or, better yet, Always Be Closing!

The Orchestra Consists of Many Parts

Just as your capital campaign consists of many parts, a fine orchestra consists of sixteen different sections. My son Matt McLaughlin, music major from Alma College, is a percussionist, and he knows what he's talking about when it comes to music. Starting in the fourth grade, he made noise with just about everything he played with. In many instances, he made lots and lots of noise. Matt is as talented playing a five-octave marimba or steel drums as he is on a drum set. I would guess that, over the years, he has played more than twenty different percussion instruments. I asked him what the most important elements of a good orchestra or band are. Without a moment's hesitation he said tune, tone, and timing.

Your capital campaign with six to ten committees/teams and fifty to one hundred volunteers is very similar to Matt's description of an orchestra. Make sure your campaign plan and case for support clearly indicate the tune, with everyone reading the same sheet of music so they will know the melody and be in tune with it (pun intended).

The second critical issue is tone. If they have the music but are off key, the sound is not very appealing. No offense to the middle school, but I remember hearing a middle school band rehearsing and then hearing the Alma College band in the same seven-day period. There was a good amount of difference in the quality of the tone and the appeal to the ear. I am not very musical, but I have sat through enough band concerts for our children to recognize quality.

You need everyone in your campaign process understanding the tune (the sheet music/the plan), but you also need everyone on pitch. All of your campaign training materials, expanded case for support, brochures, and CD's/DVD's must be totally in sync.

But perhaps the most important aspect of the orchestra is timing. Matt's percussion section, often twenty-five to fifty members strong, will wait until the exact moment to play a drum, a bell, or a cymbal. If all sixteen sections of the orchestra played at once and did not wait until their appointed time, it would be chaos. Not only would it be chaos for the conductor and members of the group, it would be even worse for those in the audience. Once again, perfect descriptions of a conundrum-free capital campaign. Each campaign committee/team and division will have an appointed time to play their role. Wise campaign counsel will help each section begin and hopefully end on time and on task.

Managing one hundred musicians is a tall task. Equally as daunting is the ongoing management of one hundred unpaid volunteers, with many somewhat unsure of their specific task in the campaign process. Not all sections of the orchestra begin and end at the same time. Not all campaign committees/teams begin and end at the same time either.

Timing is everything. A well-orchestrated capital campaign is nothing more than a series of very focused activities and events, all heading toward a common goal of meeting and exceeding campaign fulfillment.

At the next concert you attend, tune into the tone and the timing of your favorite band or orchestra. A co-nundrum-free campaign will have many of the same elements as a fine-tuned band or orchestra. Remember, it will need good sheet music (a plan, calendar, time line, etc.), a good conductor (campaign director, chief development officer, campaign committee/team chairs, etc.), and good performers (volunteers who will perform their tasks at the appointed time and help you fulfill your financial goals).

Big Picture, Same Goal

Staff, board, trustees, campaign cabinet, campaign committee/team members, volunteers, and, hopefully, even donors need to understand the rationale for your capital campaign. Why do we need to raise these additional funds and what will they allow us to accomplish? Of the three P's (program, personnel, and property) you need to underwrite with the money you are raising in your campaign, which will have the greatest impact on your current and future ministry? What are you not doing now that, as a result of your capital campaign, you want to be doing in the future?

But the bigger question is this: Does everyone involved in the campaign *see* and understand this big picture? One of the most important communication issues as you launch your public phase is to continue to communicate up and down the ranks why you are doing this campaign, so everyone understands the common goal and everyone sees and understands the big picture.

It is my understanding that conceptual thinkers make up around 11 percent of the human population. If you share a concept or vision and paint a mental picture, they get it right away and begin to see its impact. Here is a great story about Walt Disney and his vision (big picture idea) to create another theme park in Florida.

It took many years to purchase land in Orlando, Florida, build all the initial buildings and attractions, and hire and train staff before Disney World became a reality in 1979. And unfortunately, Walt Disney died before the theme park opened. At the grand opening's ribbon-cutting ceremony, one of the Disney vice presidents leaned over to Mrs. Disney and said, "I wish Walt were here to see this."

Perhaps one of the most profound statements in the history of big-picture visionaries was made when Mrs. Disney replied without hesitation, "He already saw it." She was saying that, in Walt's mind, he had already seen the most visited theme park in the world. He was one of those 11 percent of conceptual thinkers.

Don't assume all of your board, faculty, staff, campaign committee/team members, volunteers, and donors are conceptual thinkers. You will

"He already saw it."

have to continue to share the big picture needs of your organization and how this campaign will fulfill those needs. Oh, by the way, as you share the big picture, continue to share the goal. A common campaign goal that every committee/team and volunteer must understand from the get-go is to raise the money and build organizational capacity for the future.

Job Descriptions and Performance Expectations

The public phase of the campaign is when you may have five to ten campaign committees/teams active at the same time. So to avoid confusion, or in some instances nearly complete chaos, you need to present job descriptions and performance expectations to all of your campaign committees/teams.

In the last chapter we shared a very brief, 30-second job description for each of the committees/teams. Here are expanded versions. Without specific job descriptions and performance expectations, you will create conundrums. Whether you have a one-million-dollar campaign goal or a one-hundred-million-dollar campaign goal, you must use your volunteers to help accomplish your dollar goal during the public phase by being very specific with assignments, goals, and expectations. For instance, be specific about the amount of time you are asking each committee/team chair to commit to the campaign effort. I will repeat it again, volunteers do what you inspect, not what you expect.

Major/Lead Gifts

The major/lead gifts committee/team has the critical task of evaluating, cultivating, and soliciting the campaign's most important donor prospects and suspects. Eighty to 90 percent of the campaign's goal will probably come from 10 to 20 percent of your donors.

When you are specific with expectations, you get the performance desired from your lead/major gift committee/team. "We need the lead and major gift committee/team to complete personal visits with our top one hundred donor prospects and suspects in the quiet/leadership phase or fairly early in the public phase of the campaign. It is our desire that you raise $6.5 to $7 million in cash and pledges toward our $10 million goal. We will help you host four to six major-donor briefings and help you with individualized proposals to present a specific dollar request. We will ask that you meet monthly or bi-monthly to chart your progress and to hold each other accountable. When you have personally visited each prospect and suspect, we will assist you in phasing out this committee/team. Any questions?"

The following is an actual chart from a client and published here with permission. The chart defines the first seventy-four commitments toward a campaign goal of $16 million, and these are the actual size and number of commitments to date. As you can see, they are closing in on the 75 percent in cash and commitments from their high-capacity donors. Once again, I encourage you to start at the top of your donor list, not at the bottom.

CAMPAIGN COMMITMENTS	
$2,000,000	1
1,700,000	1
1,000,000	3
550,000	1
500,000	2
300,000	2
225,000	1
200,000	1
150,000	3
125,000	1
100,000	8
75,000	2
65,000	1
60,000	1
50,000	5
40,000	1
30,000	5
25,000	7
22,000	1
20,000	2
15,000	4
10,000	21
Total: $11,872,000	**74**

Spiritual Emphasis/Prayer and Praise

You invite this committee/team to help you implement the biblical mandate from Psalm 127:1 (NLT): "Unless the LORD builds a house, the work of the builders is wasted." The task set before them is to constantly bathe this campaign in prayer. Their assignment is to work with existing prayer committees/teams and expand prayer and praise opportunities. Ask them to produce a monthly prayer and praise calendar and encourage all of your various audiences to "pray without ceasing." If you are going to get serious about holistic biblical stewardship, pray before every campaign step. Oswald Chambers states it best in his book, "My Utmost For His Highest."

> To say that "prayer changes things" is not as close to the truth as saying "prayer changes me and then I change things." God has established things so that prayer, on the basis of redemption, changes the way a person looks at things.
>
> Prayer is not a matter of changing things externally, but one of working miracles in a person's inner nature."[11]

Through active prayer you will see and experience the miracles in your capital campaign. You will see it accomplished through people, hence "prayer changes me and then I change things."

After nearly three hundred capital campaigns over the past twenty eight years, I still have never caused it to rain, and I am sure I never will. But after God and His people (campaign committees/teams) get it raining, I know very well how to irrigate. Plainly stated, we want no dollar to be asked for or raised in a campaign that was not prayed over.

... "prayer changes me and then I change things."

Now, has God ever blessed us with dollars and commitments from out of left field in our campaigns (those commitments from who knows where)? Absolutely! But we place a strong emphasis upon prayer and praise in our campaigns. I have seen what I believe is literally miraculous giving in many campaigns. This committee/team is critical to success. It's not luck, ladies and gentlemen; in a good, conundrum-free campaign it's planning, hard work, committed volunteers, and lots of prayer.

Communications/Public Relations/Brand

This committee/team will help you develop your campaign theme, your logo and design—in short, your "look." Populate this committee/team with people who have print and electronic media experience. Writers, designers, and a TV or radio personality as well as anyone with experience with your local media can be helpful. Since most of us were raised in the sight-and-sound generation, you need media tools for your campaign. Yes, you will need a quality CD or DVD to help you share your story with your many donor audiences. If a picture (with sight and sound) paints a thousand words, then we need both print and electronic media to share the capital campaign story. If your website is not up to par, this committee/team could also help you upgrade your web application.

This committee/team will also create proposals for major donors, businesses, foundations, corporations, churches, and other giving sources; your campaign brochure (with lots of staff guidance); and a campaign Q & A document. Remember the mention of a political campaign and capital campaign having similar goals? That is certainly evident with this committee/team. This committee/team will help you develop the fundraising, marketing, and educational tools you need to clearly articulate your mission, vision, and core values.

Foundation Gifts

Some 217,462 foundations provided about 6 to 7 percent of the total not-for-profit, across-the-board dollars given in America last year. While foundations are selective in their giving patterns, every one of them is required to give by charter and by law. Based on the total dollars, this is not big money. But many foundations have a keen interest in capital campaigns. Of the three P's (program, personnel, and property) often associated with capital campaigns, foundations will most often support bricks and mortar because it is a solid investment of their resources. Once again this is a committee/team that will network relationships with decision makers on the foundation boards. It bears repeating: foundations do not give to proposals, but they do, in fact, give to people.

Recruit a committee/team that will know how to do research and have people with good writing and editing skills. You also want someone who knows and understands the foundation community in your local area, your region, or on a national basis. Many of these foundation requests will be made late in your campaign. In fact, one national foundation discourages you from presenting a proposal until you are at least two thirds towards fulfilling your campaign goal.

Corporation/Business

By my definition, the difference between corporations and businesses has to do with the size of the particular entity and how they are incorporated to conduct their philanthropic affairs. This team of volunteers will solicit financial contributions from local, regional, and national corporations. They will also network throughout your constituency and customer base and make requests of businesses (s-corps) and corporations (c-corps). Remember, corporations and businesses do not give to proposals, they give to people. So you will want to use relational strategy.

Who do you know and who do you need to know? Will your request need to go to corporate headquarters somewhere out of town? Or are the decision makers at a location in your city or area? This committee/team can help you research these locations and decision makers to ensure, or at least increase, your opportunity for success. They can help you become more visible in your business and corporate community. Part of the brilliance of a capital

Make all of your campaign committees/teams ...volunteer intensive...

campaign is the capacity to broaden your base of support from all levels, but certainly from these two important funding sources.

Volunteers will once again help you open these unique doors of opportunity. They personally know decision makers at the corporate level who can help you avoid the red tape and get your request considered. Volunteers can also help you meet foundation board members who once again are decision makers. Make all of your campaign committees/teams V.I. (volunteer intensive). Good volunteer participation will open doors that have never been open to you in the past.

Church Partnerships

If you are a church planning a capital campaign, then this section is not for you. If you are a parachurch organization, please take notes. I am convinced, after many years in serving both church and parachurch organizations, that there will always be an uneasy marriage between the two, but especially in this area of money (annual and capital support). In spite of the uneasiness, your conundrum-free campaign needs a church partnership division to help you network through your local, regional, or national church affiliation and/or contact base. Many colleges and other ministry organizations are able to contact their national partnership of churches, not just local. The church has the capacity to help you articulate your mission and vision (through your campaign material) and recruit volunteers and raise money, albeit various sizes and shapes of financial participation (one-time gift, monthly support, three-year commitment, freewill offering, etc.).

Probably, every board, faculty, and staff member, as well as every parent, customer, and volunteer associated with your organization has a home church. You know, the place you call home when you are going through those three critical life/family experiences: someone in your family is being hatched (birth), matched (marriage), or dispatched (funeral). Invite everyone to make a presentation to his or her own home church. They know the decision makers in their own churches, and they need to personally walk in a proposal and make a formal request. We often recommend four basic requests of our church partnership committee/team, and I'll use the fictional South Christian School in this example:

1. Ask for a special presentation Sunday at each local church (e.g., May 6 is South Christian School Sunday). Make a brief, five-minute presentation in each church with South Christian Students/Parent/Alumni representation, show a three-minute video (commercial of sorts), and read a brief, one-minute prepared statement.

2. Request the opportunity to take a freewill offering after the presentation or at the end of the service for the ongoing needs of South Christian.

3. Request the opportunity to present a proposal, inviting the church to take on a three-year commitment to the capital campaign, (e.g., $10,000 over and above the freewill offering and their regular annual support of the school).

4. Request the opportunity, or at least inform the church leadership of your intent, to visit every family in the church with a South Christian connection. You normally do not need their permission, but it is a courtesy to ask.

The most critical components of your church partner-ship committee/team are to raise the level of awareness, re-cruit students, recruit volunteers, and educate the churches in your constituency about your ministry. You may not get permission from every church, but many will partner with you if you share with them how a partnership can work and, of course, you use active church members to approach their respective churches.

General Gifts

Everyone on your mailing list should have the oppor-tunity to upgrade their commitment or to get involved fi-nancially for the very first time. This committee/team will help you make formal requests to the general population of your donor file to upgrade a general gift commitment or make a first-time general gift commitment. So they need the capacity and mindset to present your campaign needs and use a variety of methods to bring closure to these re-lationships. This is fundraising for the multitudes, and it is a necessary step in an effective, conundrum-free capital campaign.

Under staff direction, this division uses direct mail, the telephone, and large and small group events to effectively solicit every possible name in your donor file. Under the direction of a major-donor committee/team you will get a lot from a few constituents. With your general gifts com-mittee/team you will get a little from each of a lot of do-nors. A significant number of gifts for more than $100 add up. And conundrum-free campaign planning should detail a variety of fundraising activities to re-activate lapsed donors and recruit brand new donors.

Alumni

Some of you reading this book do not have an alumni association. So you have my permission to move on to the next header. Rescue missions, Salvation Army programs, etc., you are delighted your graduates (a form of alumni) are out of your program and beginning to make their way in life after addiction, destructive behavior, etc. But a typical alumni fundraising event or activity will probably not work with them.

If it fits you, however, an alumni roll call is the cornerstone of this committee/team activity. They are about asking fellow alumni to help out with a cause that should be near and dear to their hearts. I am living proof that this works. I gave a first gift to my alma mater when my former college roommate, Glenn Amos, called me during an alumni roll call and asked me to match his gift for a capital campaign.

A healthy part of the alumni division's activity is to update phone numbers, email addresses, and home mailing addresses for your alumni. A real benefit is to ask alumni/alumna to review your current list of alumni so they can help you find people you've lost track of, tell you what new jobs they have taken and where they go to church these days. Many conundrum-free campaigns have wisely used an alumni committee/team and funding project to help push their campaign toward fulfillment.

Estate Design/Planned Giving

In the stewardship business, I have been asked these questions hundreds of times: "Pat, when would you recommend we begin our planned and deferred giving program? When should we get serious about estate planning?" My answer is always the same: ten years ago! That's right, it normally takes eight to ten years for a typical planned-giving program to mature and begin producing gift income for your organization. A capital campaign is a great time to recruit, train, and empower an estate planning committee/team for your organization. Keep in perspective that this committee/team is a permanent committee/team that will continue its work long after the campaign solicitation period has concluded.

Fill this committee/team with a lawyer (preferably one who practices estate planning and understands charitable counseling) and a bank trust officer (they know wealth in a community). A CFP (certified financial planner) can also be an effective member. Many times a very wealthy donor can be a great member of this committee/team. Certainly you want your chief advancement/development officer to meet and interact with this committee/team. I heard Greg Ring, who is from a national philanthropic planned giving firm, say that somewhere in the neighborhood of $46 trillion (in mostly non-cash assets) is going to change hands from the parents of baby boomer parents to baby boomers themselves over the next eight to ten years.

Wow! If Greg is right, use your campaign as the excuse, reason, justification, or pretext to begin a ministry-wide, effective, graciously aggressive planned and deferred giving effort. You will need some help in connecting the needs of your capital campaign and your planned-giving efforts, but this could be a significant part of your future.

Gifts in Kind/Special Gifts

A capital campaign is a wonderful opportunity for non-cash gifts, often referred to as gifts in kind (GIK). These non-cash gifts could account for as much as 10 to 20 percent of your total capital campaign goal in bricks and mortar efforts. I do not want, however, to limit your thoughts to just the building. Everything from furniture to art work to equipment like telephone systems and computers has been donated through the labors of an effective GIK campaign committee/team.

Once again, I encourage you to make a "needs" list and a "wants" list. What do you really *need* in your new facility to get the job done? Or if your campaign is not for bricks and mortar (property), but for one of the other two P's (program and personnel), be realistic about what you really need. As you organize your GIK committee/team, share that needs list with them.

For your wants list, think about what you would want to see donated if staffing and dollars were not an issue. For instance, you may *want* every staff member to have a new lap top, smart phone for email, and an iPod. Now you've got it! Think outside the box and share that wants list with your GIK committee/team as well.

For building needs (property, bricks, and mortar), we

encourage you to select a general contractor (GC) or a construction manager (CM) who is willing to work with donations of goods and services. Most will, but occasionally one will not. Choose wisely based upon who will. After all, if your GIK committee/team can help you raise 15 percent of your capital campaign brick and mortar goal of $10 million with gifts in kind you have just raised $1,500,000.

Yes, we have raised those kinds of dollars working with our GIK committee/team process. A great committee/team gets very busy as you begin to shop for a GC/CM for your new facility, whether it is for a new building or renovation of an existing structure. We have a bid-letting process that has been tested in many states with both union and non-union builders, and it has worked very successfully. This committee/team has a ninety-day to six-month shelf life. But if effectively used, it can provide visibility and gift income, and open many new doors of opportunity. You will build some brand new relationships with contractors and their sub-contractors, and with furniture and technology vendors. Remember, whether you raise the resources in cash or with in-kind donations, it all pays the same for you and your campaign team.

...make a "needs" list and a "wants" list.

Parents/Grandparents

I did not give you a 30-second job description for this one in an earlier chapter. In many cases, parent and grandparent campaign education and solicitation will fit with one of the other committees/teams. If not, create a separate affinity group to help you educate and solicit this critically important group. Parents and grandparents are important customers as you are educating (university, college, seminary, graduate school, K-12 private schools, etc.) or employing (social service agency, rescue mission, sending agency for missionaries, etc.).

We have discovered that parents and grandparents are very willing participants in multi-year capital campaigns, often giving over and above their current monthly commitment to your organization. Don't be afraid to organize, educate, and launch a committee/team that will specifically target this segment of your existing donor file. If parents and grandparents are not donors, the campaign is a wonderful reason to solicit their time, talent, and financial resources to assist you in fulfilling your financial goal.

In summary, I once again encourage you to practice ergonomics (fit) in your conundrum-free planning process. Don't even attempt to recruit campaign volunteers to staff a committee/team you are not sure fits your organizational capacity. It has got to fit, and you, with the help of outside counsel, need to make it work. Volunteers are normally a key part of the success of any effective capital campaign. As your campaign committee/team members make the transition from friend raisers to fundraisers, they join you in working hard to ensure campaign fulfillment and success. The public phase of a campaign is the time to really teach, train, disciple, and use one of your most important commodities—your army or handful of volunteers (whichever fits).

7

Phase IV: The Donor-Maintenance Phase

*"Treat people as if they are what they
ought to be, and you help them to
become what they are capable of being."*
— Johann Wolfgang von Goethe

If your pre-campaign study phase takes four months, your quiet/leadership phase takes six months, and your public phase takes twelve months—hold it. Let's see. Those three phases alone have consumed the first twenty-two months of your capital campaign. Depending upon your campaign length of thirty-six, forty-eight, fifty-four months, or even sixty months, your donor-maintenance phase may be the longest phase of your campaign. But a conundrum-free campaign depends on a quality plan to keep your donors informed and lift them to even higher giving levels.

Don't Grab the Money and Run

Regardless of how much money you raise in your campaign, you will probably need to raise additional capital funds one to five years down the pike. So in the meantime work hard to maintain a good relationship with every donor of record who participated in your capital campaign. Please don't work as hard as you have worked to implement a conundrum-free campaign and then let those donors finish their commitment and drop off in their giving. Don't forget your organization has not one but three funding needs: annual/operational, capital, and endowment.

What is often missed in a campaign is a further relationship-building process to deepen donor relationships and increase the "shelf life" of every donor. What if you can implement a strategy to convert all of those new campaign donors into regular annual/operational funding donors? All of your hard work would be multiplied because you would end your capital campaign with many new annual and potential endowment funding prospects and suspects.

Let me get this out of the way, right now early in the chapter. If you grab the money from your capital campaign donors and run, you will be sorry in the short term but especially sorry in the long term. Healthy organizations have realized the importance of building lifelong relationships with their donors. They become friends, "yea verily" (slipped a little KJV in on you), they become members of your organization/ministry family.

...process to deepen donor relationships and increase the "shelf life" of every donor.

We encourage all of our clients to "date" their donors. Sounds goofy, but I can assure you after all these years of helping clients date their donors that it will build long and deep relationships. The donor-maintenance phase of your campaign is a great time to continue this dating routine. Building a lifelong relationship is not going to happen, or at least not happen as you had hoped, without a good donor-maintenance plan and process.

Remember, hope is not a strategy. It's a great comfort and a cool thing to share with each other, but it is not in and of itself a strategy. This fourth and another critical phase of your capital campaign must be worked with the same energy and attention you gave to the first three phases—pre-campaign study, quiet/leadership, and public. If you ease up and do not apply yourself to this phase of the campaign you will regret it. You have been researching, romancing, and making requests of your donors for the past twelve to eighteen months. Now you have the opportunity to drill deeper and enhance that ongoing donor relationship. Maintain, build, deepen, enhance, fine-tune, and say "thanks a zillion" to all of your donors in this critical phase of your conundrum-free capital campaign.

WD-40 for various products in your home, Mobil 1 10W-40 for your automobile, liquid graphite for your locks, and 2 cycle oil for your Weed Eater are lubricants that make those products work smoothly. Without lubrication your car will stop working, your doors will squeak, your locks will freeze up, and your Weed Eater will…well, you know.

Think of the donor-maintenance phase of your campaign as lubrication. Grease the skids for a next campaign gift with a series of steps to say thanks and further educate your donor base. Make sure you lubricate the relationship and keep it working free and easy for subsequent fundraising opportunities.

How do you lube up those donor relationships? I thought you would never ask! There are some do's and don'ts in this donor-maintenance phase, and make sure you do the do's and don't do the don'ts.

The Importance of Good Donor-Based Software

You must have excellent donor-based software to help you manage every donor relationship. Not good *accounting* software, but good *donor-based* software. Accounting software is about getting the numbers correct. Donor-based software is about building the relationship and making it work. Accounting software wants to know name, address, phone, and zip code. Donor-based software wants to know all that and oh so much more.

Knowing the names and ages of children and grandchildren is very helpful. Birthday and wedding anniversary dates are very useful pieces of information as you continue to thank donors and deepen relationships. What if you could send personalized birthday cards to key donors and thank them on behalf of your organization and, of course, wish them well on these milestones? Or send cards or emails with good wishes and congratulations on their wedding anniversaries?

Good software and a good plan allow you to maintain and enhance the relationship with both husband and wife, as you should. Check out the national statistics: Women outlive men by 7.8 years. Guess who might have the final say in a donor relationship for your organization?

Do the Do's

If you don't have good donor-based software, bite the bullet and make the purchase now, regardless of what campaign phase you're in. A number of good donor-based

Donor-based software is about building the relationship and making it work.

software products are on the market, even a couple of inexpensive web-based applications. Find some user-friendly software that will help you manage multi-year pledges. You will address potential conundrums (present and future) upfront if you will use your campaign to gather good information and build your information base. Here are some questions you should ask about your software.

1. Is it user-friendly? Is it easy to operate? Can all your staff be trained to use it?
2. Will it easily and without manipulation produce accurate, useable donor reports?
3. Does it have 24-hour support service should you need it?
4. Is it network and web-friendly?
5. Does it have good and easy data entry and a reporting system for managing personal contacts made with each donor annually?
6. Does it show a screen detailing gift history dates for each donor, including pledges, payments, capital and annual account credited, dates of pledges and payments, volunteer assignments, pledge/payment schedule, type of gift (e.g., cash, deferred, in-kind), total pledged and total paid to date on a campaign pledge, balance due, and any donor recognition name for each pledge and gift?

7. Does it give you the ability to code separate donor recognition names (e.g., husband, wife, child, business, etc.) and publicly code for each pledge and outright gift?
8. Does it have the capacity to automatically generate personalized acknowledgment letters with name, address, salutation, date, pledge amount, gift description, and payment amount?
9. Does it have a system to generate receipts and billing statements as well as pledge status and payment reports (pledge reminders/commitment updates); defining current, upcoming and delinquent payments in each donor's name and/or business name?
10. Does it generate separate capital campaign and annual fundraising segment gift totals, as well as the entire total, including lifetime giving history?
11. Does it allow you to input and report on a stock gift's net value, broker fees, and donor recognition level?
12. Does it handle the reporting on matching gifts and gifts split between spouses or family members?
13. Does it maintain as many pledges per donor as you need?
14. Does it let you locate information phonetically or by using partial names of donors, potential donors, and volunteer records through a variety of methods, including the following?
    a) File Identification Number
    b) Name (or partial name)
    c) Business/Corporation Name
    d) Donor Recognition Name(s)
    e) Constituency

f) Association (e.g., alumni, guild, society, etc.)
15. Does it allow coding prospect type and current capital campaign or annual fundraising status of an individual with a code for each of the following categories?
    a) Individual, Business (s-corp.), Corporation (c-corp.), Foundation, Other Giving Club
    b) Active, Inactive, Lapsed, Do Not Solicit
    c) Priority, Upgrade, Decline
    d) LYBNTY, SYBNTY ("last year but not this year" and "some year but not this year")
    e) Up and down relationships—children and line of family succession
    f) Ability to code salutations to generate personalized letters from your software
    g) Ability to code a prospect's gift potential
16. Does it have the ability to track each capital campaign segment's (lead gifts segment, corporation segment, foundation segment, alumni segment, etc.) volunteer hierarchy?
17. Does it have the ability to track a volunteer's goal?
18. Does it have the ability to track a volunteer's activity toward achieving that goal?
19. Does it have the ability to track a volunteer's prospect assignments?
20. Does it have the ability to track a volunteer's progress in relation to his/her individual goal?
21. Can it help you manage every special event that is planned and implemented in your campaign?
22. Does it have the ability to track each type of event and location?

23. Can it sort out the invitees, attendees, and donors for each of those special events?

24. Will you have easy access to gift history that relates to pledges and payment toward those pledges in your capital campaign?

25. Will you be able to select and sort on all code fields generating either standard donor reports or unique user-definable reports, mailing labels, word processing addresses, and salutation lists?

26. Will you have the ability to dump all information on a person/giving unit computer file in report format for use by your development/fundraising staff and volunteers?

27. Will you be able to generate estate/planned giving gift's maturities and expectancy reports based on donor birthdates to project future cash flow for your campaign?

Here are some basic information categories in checklist form to help you discover what your software has the capacity to help you manage and maintain.

❑ Name
❑ Address
❑ Salutation
❑ Additional salutations
❑ Home phone
❑ Business phone
❑ Cell phone
❑ Email address
❑ Alternative address (snow birds)

- ❏ Profiles
- ❏ Mail status (1-4-6-12 times annually)
- ❏ Church affiliation
- ❏ Date of birth
- ❏ Largest gift amount
- ❏ Largest gift date
- ❏ Largest gift motivation
- ❏ Last gift amount
- ❏ Last gift date
- ❏ Volunteer status
- ❏ Last gift motivation
- ❏ First gift amount
- ❏ First gift date
- ❏ First gift motivation
- ❏ Comments (Relationship-based software – 5 R's)
- ❏ Source date of original information

This list of donor maintenance questions and data categories is by no means exhaustive. Most software packages today allow you to customize and create reports that really hone in on information you want and need. But conundrum-free campaigns begin and end with good software. And deepening a relationship with donors begins and ends with good software, which is a must to maintain, enhance, love, and care for your donor base. Keep in perspective, however, that as high tech as you can become with your great donor software, you should not forget high touch. All the information in the world will not help you deepen and expand donor relationships; there is just one way to do that—in person and with one donor at a time.

Commitment Updates and Pledge Reminders

Stewardship is a two-way street, and you need to provide an update and reminder service to help your donors manage their multi-year commitment. First of all, discover how and when they intend to fulfill their commitment—monthly, quarterly, semi-annually, or annually is how most capital campaign pledges are paid. (Many major donors will fulfill their commitment annually and often in the fourth quarter of the year. Yes, many of these kinds of commitments are fulfilled in December and often on the 26th to the 31st.)

No reason to be shy. This affords your organization and the donor an opportunity to deepen a relationship. This donor-maintenance phase allows you to communicate progress on the donor's pledge as well as other campaign progress. Conundrum-free campaigns use the donor-maintenance phase of their campaign to collect 95-104 percent of their campaign pledges. Yes, with good donor maintenance you can collect all of your pledges and often go beyond the pledged amount.

Stewardship is a two-way street...

Julie Nicholson of Pantego Christian Academy in Arlington, Texas has a volunteer who used to call them "excuse cards" instead of pledge cards. Her experience was that people only signed a pledge card or used a letter of intent to get around giving cash they did not really intend to give. But Julie used a good pledge reminder system and went over 100 percent in pledge fulfillment in her last campaign.

Most capital campaigns have a three- to five-year donor fulfillment time line. Good software will allow you to keep your donors informed and updated on your project and where they are in the thirty-six- to sixty-month process of fulfilling their commitment. The accuracy of your data and the capability of your software will help you do a great job in your pledge reminder strategy.

We are often asked how frequently organizations should send pledge reminder/commitment updates to donors with outstanding commitments. Commitment updates are normally sent quarterly, semi-annually, and annually.

Pledges, commitments, yea verily a promise (that is what, in essence, a written pledge is) must be managed by good software and upfront communication. These updates and reminders are provided both for those who are current with their commitments and those who are delinquent. What is a delinquent donor, you ask? Good question. That will vary by the organization and sometimes even by the campaign. Usually in a capital campaign, if a commitment becomes more than six months delinquent, you need to communicate with the donor and at least find out what's going on. Campaign conundrums can develop because of poor communication, especially in this area of fulfillment.

To top it all off, pledge reminders and commitment updates are biblical. Listen to the apostle Paul's personal pledge reminder to the church in Corinth. II Corinthians 9:1-5 reads:

I really don't need to write to you about this ministry of giving for the believers in Jerusalem. For I know how eager you are to help, and I have been boasting to the churches in Macedonia that you in Greece were ready to send an offering a year ago. In fact, it was your enthusiasm that stirred up many of the Macedonian believers to begin giving.

But I am sending these brothers to be sure you really are ready, as I have been telling them, and that your money is all collected. I don't want to be wrong in my boasting about you. We would be embarrassed—not to mention your own embarrassment—if some Macedonian believers came with me and found that you weren't ready after all I had told them! So I thought I should send these brothers ahead of me to make sure the gift you promised is ready. But I want it to be a willing gift, not one given grudgingly. (NLT)

Read it again. Did you miss that passage and concept in your last reading of this epistle? Yes, this was the very first pledge reminder. The apostle Paul secured a commitment from the Greek Christians in the church at Corinth for the persecuted believers in Jerusalem. It appears Paul had been bragging about the gift to the Macedonians. Neither Paul nor the Jerusalem church had seen the gift, so Paul sent "Mr. T" (Titus), his associate at the time, and the brothers to pick up the money. I believe the brothers were converted Roman soldiers (Paul was often under house arrest) who had become believers and were committed to helping Paul.

Think about it, Paul sent Titus and these two large Roman soldiers to the home of the Corinthian church pastor to pick up the money. In our modern day this could almost be a scene from *The Godfather* movie or a clip from *The Sopranos* TV show. Can you hear a big guy with a Jersey or Roman accent say "Hey, Reverend, our buddy Paul sent us to see you. Have you got the money ready for us to deliver to our people in Jerusalem?"

...Paul sent "Mr. T" (Titus)...and the brothers to pick up the money.

That sounds humorous, but Paul was so serious he sent the collection agency to pick up the money in person. This was a personal as well as a written pledge reminder. If it worked for Paul, it will work for you. To be conundrum-free you may need to send "the brothers" to pick up a handful of delinquent commitments in your next campaign.

Visit Your Key Donors in Person

Another "do" in the donor-maintenance phase of your capital campaign is to visit all key donors in person. Invest quality time with a personal visit to the financial partners of your organization and capital campaign to just "love on them." All the data pledge reports, commitment updates, friendly emails, and the like cannot and should not replace a personal sit-down visit with your key donors to say thanks. Writing thank-you notes by hand is a lost art, and so is the art of saying a personal, look-you-in-the-eye, heartfelt thank you.

Foundations are not impersonal institutions; they are run by people you should treat like major donors. A thank you should be as personal as possible. Try to make an appointment. If that is not an option, call them on the phone. If that doesn't work, send a note. Or better yet, do some combination of the three. My colleague at The Timothy Group, Ron Haas, tells the story of a foundation director who increased his gift by seven times because the director of a ministry called to say thanks in person.

When the ministry received a $10,000 grant from this foundation that was unrelated to their capital campaign, the ministry leader asked us for suggestions for thanking the foundation. Since the foundation director was unaware of the capital campaign, we suggested that, after expressing personal thanks for the grant, the ministry leader ask if the foundation might consider the same gift annually over three years as a part of the capital campaign.

The foundation director appreciated the ministry leader's taking the time to personally say thank you, and said, "You would be surprised to know how many organizations receive a grant from us and never contact us again." Because of this hit-and-run pattern, the foundation had redesigned their grant-making policies. The foundation board would decide what size grant they were willing to give each project and then make a partial gift. If the organization thanked them and continued to cultivate a relationship, the foundation would give the rest of the gift they originally had in mind. If the organization went silent, however, so did the foundation.

"We choose whether or not to give the rest of the grant

based on how the organization follows up with us," he said. "So not only will we give you $10,000, I'll add $15,000 annually for the next three years to make a total $75,000 campaign commitment." That day the ministry leader saw a $10,000 grant turn into $75,000, all because he expressed thanks.

Jim Schlottman, former chief advancement officer for the University of Colorado Medical School, in Denver, Colorado, shared with me many years ago that a key donor in their program was thanked seven times. How much is too much? I frankly do not know. But to maintain and enhance a donor relationship you must use those familiar four-letter words: *time, love,* and *care.*

Too often we do not say thanks in an appropriate way. We do not keep the donor informed about the progress of their investment in our capital campaigns. That, friends, is a big-time mistake. That is a conundrum in the making for a future campaign if not for this one. Will you need to raise additional monies in the future? Is this the only capital campaign you will every conduct? After the campaign is fulfilled, do you still want the donor to give to your annual/ operational funding needs? Do you feel like this donor may be a candidate for a planned-giving opportunity somewhere down the road?

> *...you must use those familiar four-letter words:* time, love, *and* care.

Most of those questions can be answered in personal sit-down, educational, motivational, kind, caring, and loving conversations. They do not have to be lengthy meetings, but don't rush the conversation. This is a great opportunity to share, update, thank your donors in person, ask for prayer requests if appropriate, and close in prayer. Thank God for them and for the progress made in the campaign to date. While we all agree high tech is important, there is absolutely no substitute for high touch.

Practice the Golden Rule

How would you like to be thanked for a gift? How do you want to be treated in a donor relationship? These questions are a good way to think through the donor maintenance policy at your organization.

I was at a stewardship conference in Coventry, England, teaching a session on donor relationships for a group of about ninety Christian leaders from England, Ireland, Scotland, and Wales. As mentioned before, my five R's for major-donor plans are Research, Romance, Request, Recognition and Recruitment. When I got to the Recognition segment (saying thank you and deepening the relationship with a donor), the vicar from a Church of England parish asked, "Pat, in this room is a ministry organization that received a gift of 10,000 pounds eighteen months ago and to date our parishioner has not received a thank-you note, receipt, or an acknowledgement. Is that normal?"

Based on the Golden Rule or even the rule of commonsense, I quickly replied no. In US currency that is a gift of $18,000. None of us would want to be treated in that manner for a gift of even $18.00. I encouraged that delinquent organization to seek out the vicar to do a little old-fashioned donor maintenance and visit that donor in person. I encouraged them to also hand deliver a receipt and acknowledgment and to ask the donor to forgive them for this grave oversight.

In short, say thanks and really mean it. How do you do that, you ask? Now come on, be a little bit creative and work up a plan that is appropriate and fits you and your organization. If you will carefully and prayerfully maintain relationships with your donors you will build lifelong loyalty and increase their capacity to give with every capital campaign you conduct. Practice the Golden Rule with your donors and it will pay off. In fact, it will pay off in additional gold being shared with your organization. It will also help you avoid that conundrum of a shrinking donor base for your capital campaign. Wisely use your donor-maintenance phase to expand the time, talent, and treasure your donors invest in your organization.

8

The Role of the Board in Your Conundrum-Free Campaign

"The final test of a leader is that he leaves behind him in other men, the conviction and the will to carry on."
— *Walter Lippmann*

By now the secret is out. There are very few conundrum-free capital campaigns. Somewhere in the process a conundrum emerges and slows or impedes progress. Good planning will help you quickly address or, in some instances, eliminate the conundrum.

But let's get this out of the way right now. Without trustee/board financial participation and without their ownership you are virtually guaranteed conundrums. "Why?" you ask. Let me see if I can deliver a bit of wisdom

I've gleaned over the past twenty eight years in the fund-raising/stewardship/capital campaign business.

In a "What's Working in Non-Profit Fundraising" April 1994 article, it was revealed that fewer than 30 percent of board members are formally required to give, even though everyone knows it's important for all board members to support their nonprofit's fundraising efforts. The article went on to say the reasons CEOs did not require board giving was that many (1) felt it would scare away candidates who could help the organization without donating money, (2) thought board members were recruited for their skills and that their input could benefit the 501(C)3 far more than money they might give, and (3) were concerned that affluent board members might think they've been recruited for their pocketbooks rather than for their input.

The three reasons the article listed for having a "required giving policy" were:

1. A board giving policy is a sure way to get 100 percent compliance. Boards, foundations, corporations, and individual donors like to know directors are donors, that those helping to govern the organization are financial partners.
2. A board giving policy helps to ensure the organization's financial health. In the current economic climate, board giving is absolutely essential to the health of many non-profit organizations.
3. A board giving policy discourages people who want to sit on a nonprofit board simply for the prestige and recognition.[12]

Please allow me to summarize this article and survey very quickly. In fact, I will use the wise words of a first-century Internal Revenue Service agent to help me. His name was Matthew, and he was a tax collector who knew a good bit about money. "Wherever your treasure is, there the desires of your heart will also be" (Matthew 6:21 NLT).

Do you want and need the hearts and thoughts of your board members in a capital campaign? Pat's survey says absolutely. You want commitment of time, talent, skills, and input from your board of directors. Make sure you sign them up as donors to your organization. I could not state it any more clearly than the first-century tax collector, Matthew.

The Role of the Board—in Threes and Fours

These gems come from our Timothy Group training manual for not-for-profit boards.

THE THREES

As we teach, train, and disciple board members in a capital campaign, we teach in threes. You need these three levels of engagement from your board or trustees: their work, wisdom, and wealth—or time, talent, and treasure. You need their influence, affluence, and their time. You would love a board member to invest all three elements in your conundrum-free capital campaign; you may have to settle for just two of the three. But ask your board to step up and lead in these critical areas.

THE FOURS

Management of an NGO-501 (C) 3 is a partnership between the board/trustees and the professional staff. An NGO board needs to know that it owns the organization not for its own sake but for the sake of the mission that organization is to fulfill. They own it because they care and are committed to see that organization advance. As promised, here is the function of the board in four specific arenas.

BOARD MEMBERS ARE...

1. GOVERNORS — As policy makers and trustees they govern the organization. Issues of polity and policy are theirs to direct.

2. AMBASSADORS — They interpret the mission, vision, and core values of the organization.
They defend it when it is under pressure from internal or external forces. They represent it to their constituencies and communities. They are noisy about their favorite charity (in a positive way).

3. CONSULTANTS — Board members bring professional skills that would be expensive if you had to pay for them. They

can lend the years of decision-making experience and counsel they have learned in their own work-a-day world.

4. SPONSORS — Board members have an active role in giving money and helping to raise funds. They should give in proportion to their means. Not equal giving but equal sacrifice, and their giving should be a high priority to your organization.

In a conundrum-free capital campaign you will need your board to invest all or most of the aforementioned groupings of three and four functions.

Board Members

The Buck Starts and Stops with the Board

A capital campaign is a taxing experience for nearly every organization regardless of the size of its development staff. Managing donor lists, creating material, planning special events, creating calendars and time lines, and, most of all, making personal solicitation visits, are just a handful of the tasks needed in a campaign. This whole process—from strategic plan through pre-campaign study, quiet/leadership, public, and donor-maintenance phases—must be owned by your board of trustees. The beginning and the end of your campaign will need board input, participation, and ownership.

All along the way they will need to help you implement and occasionally tweak your campaign strategy. From the get-go your board needs to help the organization focus on those critical elements of mission, vision, and core values. The board needs to ask how this campaign will help your organization be more efficient and effective, how the monies raised in this campaign will help increase your ministry capacity. The board of your organization has to help you be mission-driven in your campaign, not project-driven.

The board of your organization has to help you be mission-driven in your campaign, not project-driven.

The need to fund projects will come and go but the mission of your organization will be an ongoing, lasting element. So the "buck" does not just stop with your board of trustees (the old Harry S. Truman saying—"the buck stops here"), it also starts with them. Make sure your board is committed to your entire campaign process.

Those Who Ask Must Give First

The first target group in your campaign is your board and advisory board. Once again, they must step up first. As we approach philanthropy and stewardship in the year 2010 and beyond, board-giving is a must. What if you asked your board to be responsible for one third of your capital campaign financial goal?

They could do this through their own giving or by encouraging others to give (their friends, family, business associates, foundations, corporations, etc.). This could eliminate most capital campaign conundrums. There would be the guarantee of ownership, and there would be new donor acquisition as they invited their friends, family, and colleagues to give to your effort.

Foundations who contribute about five to six cents of the non-profit dollar giving each year in America have become very sophisticated at asking the hard questions as you solicit them for funds. They often ask about the giving levels and participation of your "immediate family" (board, faculty, staff); "family" (customers, students, parents, service users, close friends, alumni); "constituency" (donors, friends, mailing list, etc,); and then the "community" (those in your city, town, village, region, universe). One of the first questions is usually about your board participation, and if you cannot answer that question to their satisfaction, you are unlikely to secure funds.

If you intend to get your board involved in making financial requests early in your campaign, you need to solicit their commitments first. Yes, you need to seek and secure 100 percent participation from your board.

Individuals Are the Target and Just a Few Fund the Biggest Percentage of Your Goal

Also early in your campaign, help your board members understand that foundations and corporations account for only around ten cents on the

...you need to seek and secure 100 percent participation from your board.

dollar in a campaign. Eighty cents or more will be given by individuals. In my twenty eight years of speaking to a hundred boards a year, I continue to be amazed at how many of them encourage their campaign team to chase after foundation and corporate dollars.

Certainly this should be a part of your comprehensive campaign strategy, but encourage your board to invest significant time in individual donors in your community. That's where the real money is, and you must use your board relationships to open those doors of opportunity.

If 80 percent of your campaign dollars is going to be given by 20 percent of your constituency, then invest time with individuals. In some campaigns these days, 90 percent of the gifts are contributed by 10 percent of the constituency. You are usually only a relationship or two away from the major contributors in your campaign. Since we already know the number one reason people give is because of who asks, your board needs to help you research, romance, and make requests to high-capacity individuals in your universe.

Fun Raising, Friend Rising, and Fundraising

Let's close out this chapter with some practical ways to involve your board in your conundrum-free capital campaign.

Major Donor Introductions: Major-donor prospects and suspects to your capital campaign do not give to proposals, they give to people—especially to those they know and trust. Board members can play an important role in opening these doors as "friend raisers." These calls are most effective when the board member can accompany the staff or campaign volunteer on the donor visit. Early in the campaign every board member needs to make a list of potential major donors they think would sit down and listen to the campaign/ministry story.

Campaign/Ministry Briefings: A capital campaign is a good opportunity to invite each board member to host a small group ministry briefing. The purpose of the briefing is to introduce their friends and associates to the ministry and share the components of the campaign. These events are often conducted in the home of the board member, with four to six couples. No funds are solicited at the event; each giving unit that attends will be asked to schedule a personal follow-up visit with a ministry representative and in many instances the board member. The half-hour meeting is to encourage each donor or donor couple to consider their financial involvement in the campaign.

Local Church Presentations: Board members can help enhance church giving in your campaign. Granted, one of the toughest places in America to raise money is the local church. Often the wrong person makes the request to the church missions committee/team, like the executive director, CEO, president, or development/advancement officer. A request by someone the church does not know is a tough sell.

Churches complain that they get too many requests for their capacity to give. Our experience confirms, however, that a one- or three-year request made by a board member of their own church's governing body (pastor, deacons, elders, mission committee/team) is often granted. We have seen nearly 40 percent of those personal, insider requests granted. The home church of every board and staff member should be personally invited to become a donor to your capital campaign.

Foundation/Corporation/Business Request: None of these three funding sources give to proposals, they give to people. These sources contribute—sometimes very generously—to organizations and people they perceive are making a difference in the world. A capital campaign is an excellent way to introduce or re-engage these funding sources. Since people give to people, your board can play a key role in opening a door of opportunity with one or all three of these sources. If one of your board members is personally acquainted with a decision maker, that's a great way to help ensure success in the solicitation process.

Remember to practice the five R's with your board with these sources: careful research; a good romance visit (to determine their specific area of interest) with a ministry representative along to help share the story; a request made in person by the board member, not by mail or by telephone; a heartfelt and meaningful recognition/thank you process; and, when possible, the recruitment step in the donor cycle, enlisting the help of the funding source with their friends.

Thank-You-Thon: We invite every client running a capital campaign to provide the names and phone numbers of their donors to their board members at a late October or early November board meeting. (If the donors are thinking about a year-end gift, then you may be already on their minds.) When you have them all together you can do a bit of training as well.

We provide a prepared script and invite them to call a full or partial list of donors or at least high-capacity donors to say thank you over the next three- to four-week period. There is no request for funding; it is just a simple "thank you" telephone visit. Often the call is only two to five minutes in length with scripted talking points about the year in ministry. A heartfelt thanks from a trustee/board member is a great way to deepen the relationship with your donor base. We ask each board member to make a minimum of ten telephone calls. Just two to three calls a week with perhaps fifteen minutes of talk time goes a long way to enhance donor relations. They close the call by asking for any prayer requests from the donor and then they pass those along to the staff. The donor's needs are prayed for in a staff/board meeting and the donor gets a handwritten note saying their special need was prayed for. Pray for your donors.

WOW, you say. I totally agree. This is an awesome way to get your board and donors talking about your organization and presents a ministry opportunity for your board.

Hand Deliver Receipts: During the course of a capital campaign, hand delivering a closed-faced receipt/thank you letter (closed-faced so the board member does not know the amount) is another great way to make your effort conundrum-free. This personal touch for any gifts over $1,000, $10,000, or $100,000—you decide on an amount—is a significant way to enhance and cultivate a relationship with a donor. If receipts/thank yous are distributed geographically, this could take only fifteen to thirty minutes per month.

Hear it again, in our high tech world this is definitely a high touch experience for your donors and your board. We often ask each board member to hand deliver fifteen to twenty receipts/thank yous a year during the course of your three years of campaign fulfillment.

Pray for your donors.

The conversation is usually at the front door and only lasts a few moments. If you want to stand out from the other organizations in your service area, making personal telephone calls and hand-delivering receipts/thank yous will set you apart.

A proactive board is an effective board. It's not just policy and governance; there is also an element of partnership with ministry leadership and the capital campaign team.

You will discover which board members are truly committed with their work, wisdom, and wealth by the use of their affluence, their influence, and their time.

I firmly believe if they are too busy to work they may be too busy to properly govern. By involving your board in your conundrum-free capital campaign you will increase their vision for your ministry and will create a very positive team spirit among your staff, administration, and campaign volunteers. Campaigns are hard work, but by involving your board members, you lighten the load and expand your capacity to minister to your donors.

9

Conundrum-Free Campaigning with Your Volunteers

"Leadership is not something you do to people, it's something you do with people." — *Ken Blanchard*

"Union gives strength." — *Aesop*

How would little league baseball take place without volunteers? How would soup kitchens or after-school programs fare?

It is estimated that just over 8.2 billion hours of volunteer time were invested in all kinds of organizations in America in 2006, with an estimated value of $152 billion. According to a July 9, 2007, *USA Today* article, middle-class Americans volunteer the most. Minneapolis, Salt Lake

City, Austin, Omaha, and Seattle had the highest volunteer ratios; 40.5 percent of Minneapolis residents volunteered time in 2006. Cities that ranked the lowest were New York, Miami, and Las Vegas (see chart below), says a report put out in July 2007 by the Corporation for National and Community Service.

Metro Areas with the most helping hands.

The 50 metropolitan areas with the highest percentage of residents ages 16 and older who volunteered in 2006

Rank	Metro Area	Pct.	Rank	Metro Area	Pct.
1	Minneapolis-St. Paul	40.5%	26	Baltimore	28.6%
2	Salt Lake City	38.4%	27	Albuquerque	27.8%
3	Austin	38.1%	28	Indianapolis	27.7%
4	Omaha	37.8%	29	Richmond, Va.	27.6%
5	Seattle	36.3%	30	Boston	27.5%
6	Portland, Ore.	35.8%	31	Cleveland	27.5%
7	Kansas City	34.9%	32	Chicago	27.4%
8	Milwaukee	34.4%	33	San Jose, Calif.	27.4%
9	Charlotte	34.3%	34	Detroit	27.0%
10	Tulsa	33.7%	35	San Antonio	26.7%
11	Cincinnati	33.4%	36	Philadelphia	26.6%
12	Columbus, Ohio	33.3%	37	Sacramento	26.5%
13	Pittsburgh	32.6%	38	Atlanta	26.1%
14	Bridgeport, Conn.	32.3%	39	Tampa	25.8%
15	Washington	31.9%	40	Houston	25.8%
16	Louisville	31.6%	41	Phoenix	23.5%
17	Denver	31.5%	42	Honolulu	23.3%
18	St. Louis	30.9%	43	Providence	23.3%
19	Nashville	30.5%	44	Los Angeles	22.3%
20	Dallas	30.3%	45	Orlando	22.2%
21	Oklahoma City	30.3%	46	Riverside, Calif.	20.6%
22	New Haven, Conn.	30.2%	47	Virginia Beach	19.3%
23	Hartford, Conn.	29.6%	48	New York	18.7%
24	San Francisco	29.6%	49	Miami	16.1%
25	San Diego	29.2%	50	Las Vegas	14.4%

Source: *Volunteering in America:2007 City Trends and Rankings* by the Corporation for National and Community Service.

How effective could your ministry be and in particular how effectively could your capital campaign function with quality, thoroughly trained, strategically placed volunteers? You have a much better chance of conduct-

You have a much better chance of conducting a successful, totally fulfilled, conundrum-free capital campaign with the wise use of top-notch volunteers.

ing a successful, totally fulfilled, conundrum-free capital campaign with the wise use of top-notch volunteers.

A Volunteer Invites Others to Volunteer

Allow me to share a letter and information from the campaign chair of one of the campaigns we have underway in the state of Ohio. The letter and information is part of a volunteer recruitment brochure, and it goes like this:

Dear Friend of MCS

Thanks for reading this brochure. I take this to mean you are interested in the school and the plans to build an Early Childhood wing on the present facility (a school with about 700 students P-K-12). This critical component of MCS's future provides opportunity for continued growth not only at the early childhood level, but throughout the grades as younger children grow older and continue through high school graduation.

A capital campaign is the most effective way to

realize the funds needed for ministry expansion. The reason for that is the active participation of volunteers. We anticipate that 75 or more volunteers will be a part of the "Igniting Young Minds" campaign. I hope that your prayerful consideration to be one of those volunteers will result in your participation on one of the campaign committees/teams.

The impact of volunteers in a campaign is tremendous. Not only are the tasks and responsibilities of the campaign effectively accomplished, but the opportunity to network into new contacts as a result of the volunteer relationships will have an influence upon MCS for years to come.

I encourage you to join me and many others who are volunteering to impact our community and beyond through this critical ministry of Christian education. Thanks for your consideration.

Sincerely,
Tom Freund
Campaign Chair

Tom, an owner of a local CPA firm, went on in the brochure to describe the various ways people could help. He listed seven different campaign committees/teams, and here is his description:

- Major/Lead Gifts—Identifying and speaking with key donors
- General Gifts—Organizing fundraising events
- Special Gifts—Soliciting in-kind gifts of goods and services

- Spiritual Emphasis—Praying and encouraging others to pray
- Church Relations—Making MCS presentations in area churches
- Corporate/Foundation Gifts—Cultivating and requesting gifts or grants
- Estate and Gift Design—Promoting planned-giving opportunities

For those who did not feel they could serve on a committee/team and invest eight to ten hours a month, Tom included these options:

- Invite friends to a fundraising event
- Invite friends to your home to meet a representative from MCS and hear a presentation regarding their partnership in the campaign
- Assist in organizing a prayer team
- Open your home for a capital campaign focus group discussion/fellowship

His final thoughts in this volunteer recruitment brochure were:

Volunteer Expectations: Volunteers are a very important part of a successful campaign. YOU are the means by which the ministry message will be known. It is a responsible position with significant expectations.

Support Expectations: To assist you, MCS will present information and materials designed to provide the most effective communication.

- You will learn of the ministry focus and resource needs

and have the opportunity to make a stewardship response to the school.

- You will receive orientation and training in the responsibility of your campaign team and/or area of volunteer service.
- You will be provided direction, training support, and material to be used in the process of fulfilling campaign committee/team plans.

Outcome Expectations: The outcome of your active involvement has eternal significance.

- Personal fulfillment from active participation in the mission and ministry of MCS.
- Satisfaction from a personal involvement in the attainment of a financial goal of the campaign and the realization of the Early Childhood wing.
- Participation in the process of introducing new friends to the importance of this ministry.
- Active involvement that promises to be uplifting and filled with enjoyment through the celebration of life in Jesus Christ.

Great job, Tom! Have you been that upfront and straightforward with your volunteers?

Job Descriptions

Remember, volunteers do what you inspect, not what you expect. Some of the best and worst campaign decisions often surround the recruitment and deployment of campaign volunteers. The most difficult person to dismiss from a position in your organization and campaign is a volunteer.

Tom asked people to join the campaign at Mansfield but he even went a step further and let them know the staff, board, and campaign team would provide job descriptions and training. Please, promise me right now that you will not recruit a campaign volunteer without giving him or her clear, written expectations. Yes, a job description.

> *Remember, volunteers do what you inspect, not what you expect.*

Much of our campaign manual is comprised of job descriptions, performance expectations, calendars, and time lines. It has been designed and re-designed over the years to help the volunteer be more efficient and effective. Certainly staff will oversee the volunteers, but you must have well-trained and empowered volunteers to conduct a conundrum-free capital campaign.

Recruit the Brightest and the Best

This old saying is probably just as accurate today as it was when I entered the capital campaign business: Want something done? Ask a busy person to do it. We all know that recruiting volunteers in our busy 2010-and-beyond world, however, is a daunting task. Many people would much rather write a check than volunteer their time. In fact, for some in this new millennium, time is more valuable than money. Put a different way, they have more money—at least from their perspective—than they have time.

In spite of that, conundrum-free campaigns have volunteer involvement regardless of the size of development/advancement office staff. Volunteers can open doors of opportunity it may take your staff years to open. Volunteers can take you to visit people you would never otherwise get to visit in person. Volunteers can help you expand your campaign capacity by providing help with the human (volunteer and people) and financial (cash and commitments) resources you need to be successful.

Start at the top by recruiting the brightest and the best volunteers. Don't make the mistake of deciding for them by saying "Oh, Pat is way too busy to help on this campaign. He flies all over the world." That is true, but please let yours truly decide for himself if he can find the time to serve on your campaign team.

Here is another example from Steve Wilson, advancement director for Lakeland Christian School in central Florida. Steve is in the public phase of a $27,000,000 campaign. This effort is nine times that of the smallest goal in the school's fifty-five-year history. Steve took the concept to "recruit the brightest and the best" to heart. In fact, he may have perfected it. Here is his take on their campaign as they close in on $20,000,000 million in cash and pledges.

"Pat, having a good plan, a great case for support, and a true sense of urgency (with waiting lists for admission in almost every grade), we have recruited a campaign team of over fifty volunteers." He has recruited the city attorney, the owner of a $60 million-a-year business, and the owner of one of the largest Ford dealerships in the southeast US, to name a few. Steve is convinced he has a great opportunity to be successful because he has recruited winners. These volunteers have placed their personal and professional reputations on the line with Lakeland Christian School. "Winning is a part of these volunteers' DNA," Steve went on to share. "These folks are not about failure but about winning." The brightest and the best are helping Steve succeed in central Florida.

FAT Is the Best Definition for Quality Volunteers

In chapter 3, I suggested you look in this chapter for more information, and think FAT. Well, here's what that's all about.

Go ahead, ask almost any volunteer, or for that matter any person in America, if they want to ask people for money. The quick reply is almost always no! It is often a very firm no at that. You can truly impact your campaign, however, by recruiting volunteers who fit the FAT profile. FAT is an acronym for *faithful, accessible,* and *teachable*—three key attributes you should look for in your campaign volunteers.

"F" is for faithful. Recruit volunteers who have already proven themselves to be faithful to your organization. Start by making sure they are donors. The book of Matthew makes it clear: "Wherever your treasure is, there the desires of your

> *FAT is an acronym for Faithful, Accessible, and Teachable.*

heart will also be" (Matthew 6:21 NLT). Faithful donors invest their time, their talent, and their treasure in your organization and campaign. Those are the individuals you want to recruit for your campaign committees and teams.

"A" is for accessible. Recruit volunteers who will make your organization, your campaign meetings, and activities a priority. We all do what we want to do with our time. So recruit those key volunteers who will make every campaign meeting an opportunity to help make your effort successful. If you constantly get the ol', "I am sorry but I am just too busy to help out and make campaign meetings," they are not accessible and they are not good choices.

"T" is for teachable. After all, fundraising is an art, not a science, and can be taught and caught. You want volunteers who are willing to be

> *The art of asking is a teachable activity.*

taught. They are willing to step outside of their comfort zones and learn how to ask for money. They are willing to be taught how to properly network with their friends, business associates, fellow parishioners, and the like. What can you teach a corporate executive or a successful professional person? A ton. You can teach them that they won't lose their friends if they ask them for a three-year capital campaign gift. I continue to be amazed at corporate executives who can close multi-million-dollar deals but have trouble asking their best friends for even a dollar let alone $10,000 or more for your campaign. Recruit volunteers who are willing to be taught and discipled in the area of stewardship. The art of asking is a teachable activity.

What Are Volunteers?

This is an old description of volunteers from the 1980's. You will notice some of the slogan examples are a bit out-dated but the spirit of the statement is still true:

Volunteers are like Ford Motor Company
They have better ideas

Volunteers are like Coca-Cola
They are the real thing

Volunteers are like Delta
They are ready when you are

Volunteers are like Pepsi
They have a lot to give

Volunteers are like Dial Soap
They care more

Volunteers are like VO5 hair spray
Their goodness holds in all kinds of weather

Volunteers are like Hallmark Cards
They care enough to give their very best

Volunteers are like Standard Oil
You expect more and you get it

BUT MOST OF ALL...

Volunteers are like Frosted Flakes
They're GRRREEEAAATTT!!!!!!!!!!!!!!!!!!

—Author Unknown

I use that outdated description of volunteers to remind us that volunteers were great in the 80's and are great in the 2010 and beyond. You have a much better opportunity to conduct a conundrum-free, successful campaign with the wise and prudent use of volunteers.

10

The Conundrum-Free Prescription

"For you know that when your faith is tested, your endurance has a chance to grow." James 1:3 (NLT)

"We never know how high we are till we are called to rise; and then, if we are true to plan, our statures touch the skies." — Emily Dickenson

Dr. David Blair has been our family physician since 1986, but ours is not the usual doctor-patient relationship.

Dave is a personal friend. Our wives, Jane and Cheryl, are accountability partners. Yet he has walked us through everything from the sniffles to plastic surgery with one son to ACL knee surgery with the other son to my colon issues. He has been there with good advice, bringing in specialists when needed, and has written hundreds of prescriptions for us.

A key to Dr. Blair's success is that he always starts with a diagnosis. Using his experience, he first determines what is wrong and then seeks a remedy. The cure may require a prescription, a visit to a specialist, some kind of medical therapy, or all of three. But he is practicing medicine, which is just that—an ongoing practice. Dave has seen most symptoms sometime before in his thirty-year practice, but he knows how to address each unique patient's specific ailments to find a potential cure.

On one occasion I was in the Pittsburgh airport and quite ill. I called Dr. Blair and told him my symptoms. He had me breathe heavily on the phone four to five times (not cool with those standing around me at a bank of pay telephones) and then said I had bronchitis. He called in a prescription to a local drug store near the airport, I jumped in a cab and retrieved it, and finished my road trip.

Since 1981 I have been in the practice of stewardship, a practice over the years of trial and some error (conundrums) in helping more than fifteen hundred clients achieve success in their capital campaigns. Like Dr. Blair, The Timothy Group recognizes that every client is unique. But we have also observed symptoms over the years and know how to prescribe a cure. For the most part our trial-and-error days are over. We tweak this or that, but our campaign plans have worked successfully in the US, Canada, the UK, Europe, the Middle East, and New Zealand.

By now I hope you have digested some of the recommendations we have shared to avoid or repair those campaign conundrums. But I want to give you a simplified strategy for a conundrum-free campaign.

A Time-Tested Prescription

Here is the true C factor, or the common cure for your capital campaign conundrums:

$$Rx + DR + GP + CV + HW + PG = CFC$$

Rx: Just like for Dr. Blair, it is important that you start with an accurate *diagnosis*. If you do not get the correct campaign diagnosis you will probably not get the correct prescription for a cure. My physician would not prescribe an aspirin for pneumonia. The Rx factor in your campaign is an honest evaluation of the conundrum. Next comes prescribing for the cure. The diagnosis may be easy, but the cure may be a good bit more painful. Most campaigns with multi-conundrums evident in their strategy and structure can be fixed with the right plan of action. Make sure you get the right diagnosis, and then carefully and prayerfully apply the remedy without which a cure is not easily achieved.

DR: *Donor research* is a key to lining up the human and financial resources you need for a conundrum-free campaign. Remember, all you need to be successful are donors who will give over and above their current level of giving toward your capital project, often with a multi-year gift. You also need people/volunteers, the human resources that will help you open new doors of opportunity.

I believe you can garner both of those critical resources with good donor research in a pre-campaign study, and perhaps even some in-depth donor research like Target America or Blackbaud Analytics. Find out all you can about your donor prospects and suspects prior to launching your conundrum-free campaign. If you ask good empirical questions you are likely to get good answers.

Conundrum Free Campaign

RX + DR + GP + CV + HW + PG = CFC

GP: You will need a *good plan* to work out your conundrums. Just like when Dr. Blair calls in a specialist, convince your board you need an experienced campaign consultant to help you be successful. No plan, no performance, no production. You need a strategy and structure that is time-tested, that has worked many times before. Experienced campaign counsel can bring you a plan you can tweak and put to work immediately to address your campaign conundrums. Better yet, *start out* with campaign counsel, which will help you avoid many of the conundrums upfront. Search out and select a ministry partner to walk with you through the shallow and deep waters of a campaign.

CV: *Committed Volunteers* are another part of the common cure. We are under contract with a university with over twenty employees in their advancement office. In spite of that, we recommended a national capital campaign with over fifty volunteer positions. Volunteers can help create conundrums at times, but they can also help you achieve your campaign goal quicker. We are involved with a campaign that will bulk up to over a hundred campaign volunteers as they roll out one of their campaign phases this fall. They are worth the price of admission; key volunteers are a part of a conundrum-free campaign. Provide job descriptions and hold them accountable. And while you may occasionally take one step backward managing volunteers, you should also be able to take two to three steps forward.

> *No plan, no performance, no production.*

HW: If you have not figured it out by now, understand that a capital campaign is *hard work.* Just because you have a great capital campaign cause does not mean it will get funded. Many a conundrum has developed because board members thought staff was going to do the campaign work, staff thought volunteers were going to do it, and administration thought key donors were going to do it. STOP! It's a total team effort and it is hard work. You will probably need a full-time staff person to invest forty to fifty hours per week in your campaign. You will need volunteers investing eight to ten hours per month in your campaign. Your CEO will need to invest 50-75 percent of his or her time in your capital campaign. It's hard work, but the work can be accomplished by spreading it out and getting after it. "Many hands make for light work," so says the book of Proverbs.

PG: I hope you recognize the ultimate force in a conundrum-free capital campaign. Here you go, I believe it's the *power of God.* "You are the God of great wonders! You demonstrate your awesome power among the nations" (Psalm 77:14 NLT). As good as your entire conundrum-free planning is, do not minimize the power of God in doing miracles and wonders in your capital campaign.

If you do not believe that is necessary, call or email me. I can tell you about project after project where the only conclusion we can draw is that God chose to bless beyond our wildest dreams. Remember our recommendation for a prayer and praise/spiritual emphasis team to pray and share praises of God's goodness as those prayers are answered. "Faith without works is dead." Once again, it's the prayer and hard work that lead to conundrum-free campaigns.

CFC: Is a totally *conundrum-free campaign* a real possibility? I answered that question earlier and I will answer it again, Yes, no, and maybe! Oh, stop with the wishy-washy answer. No, I am serious. I think all three of those answers are valid. It all depends upon your project, your research, the passion for your project, hard work, God's blessing, and a whole host of other factors. There is also the opportunity to take the principles you have just learned and fix the existing conundrums in your current capital campaign.

So, that's the prescription. Now let's wrap this up.

Conclusion

A conundrum or two does not mean your campaign is unsuccessful. Quite the opposite, conundrums have little to do with campaign fulfillment. They just mostly take the fun out of everything and increase the energy necessary to succeed. But you can minimize the conundrums and manage them by applying the principles shared in this book. By understanding the issues you can conduct a nearly conundrum-free campaign.

"To err is human. To really mess up takes a computer." Well, allow me to concentrate on the first part of that quote. We humans make errors, we miss deadlines, we offend donors, and we produce campaign documents with mistakes. Stuff just flat out happens; it is a reality of life. Attached to that stuff is a conundrum or two . . . or maybe even twenty-two. But by carefully planning your work, then working your plan, you have a good chance of being conundrum-free.

You know by now that after more than three hundred capital campaigns the men and women of The Timothy

Group understand the issues; we have seen the good, the bad, and the ugly in the capital-campaign process. Trust me, it's all out there in the Christian marketplace we serve. Now it's time for action.

You, or you and the team of people who have read this book, need to drive the process by either planning for a

The cure is common.

conundrum-free campaign or beginning tomorrow to apply the cure for the conundrums

in your current campaign. No finger pointing, no nasty emails. Just draw a line in the sand and decide how and how soon you will address those campaign conundrums.

Will it be fun? Nope. Will it be easy? It will not. But will it pay great dividends in human and financial resources? Absolutely! A phrase I often use to describe the labors of The Timothy Group is "Stewardship wisdom delivered." Here is a bit of that wisdom for you to apply.

God bestowed a supernatural gift of knowledge upon Solomon, as that was his one request, just as God provided knowledge and understanding to his father David. "All this," David said, "I have in writing from the hand of the LORD upon me, and he gave me understanding in all the details of the plan." The Scripture continues as David speaks to his son Solomon, "Be strong and courageous, and do the work. Do not be afraid or discouraged, for the LORD God, my God, is with you. He will not fail you or forsake you until all the work for the service of *(enter your ministry name here)* is finished" (I Chronicles 28:19-20 NIV).

The cure is common and right there at your fingertips. Common, though no capital campaign is easy. Do you truly want a conundrum-free capital campaign? Sure you do. We all do. Then go for it, because He wants you to be conundrum-free and succeed in funding and building your ministry and His kingdom.

Sources

1. McLaughlin, Patrick G. 2006. "Major Donor Game Plan: Rounding 3rd and Heading Home." Grand Rapids, MI, The Timothy Group Publishing.

2. Worth, Michael J. 2002. "New Strategies For Educational Fund Raising." Westport, CT, Praeger/Greenwood.

3. Hofstadter, Richard & Smith, Wilson. 1961. "American Higher Education." Chicago, IL, University of Chicago Press.

4. Sears, Jesse B. 1990. "Philanthropy in the History of American Higher Education." Piscataway, NJ, Transaction Publishers.

5. Sears, Jesse B. 1990. "Philanthropy in the History of American Higher Education." Piscataway, NJ, Transaction Publishers.

6. Sears, Jesse B. 1990. "Philanthropy in the History of American Higher Education." Piscataway, NJ, Transaction Publishers.

7. Oliver, Frank H. 1999. "Fellow Beggars: The History of Fund Raising Campaigning in U.S. Higher Education." PhD. Dissertation, Columbia University.

8. Havighurst, Walter. 1958. "The Miami Years, 1809-1959." New York, NY, Putnam.

9. "Tiny Wake Forest Turns Its Size Into an Asset." Andy Gardner. USA Today. October 25, 2006.

10. Slott, Ed. 2004. "Parlay your IRA into a Family Fortune." New York, NY, Penguin Group (USA) Inc.

11. Chambers, Oswald. 1963. "My Utmost For His Highest." Grand Rapids, MI, Discovery House Publishers.

12. "What's Working in Non-Profit Fundraising." April, 1994.